353.03 Radding, Charles
RAD
The modern
presidency

DATE			
OCT 1 9 '83			

The Modern Presidency

THE MODERN PRESIDENCY

Charles Radding

American Government Series

Consulting Editor, Richard Darilek

Department of History,
Herbert H. Lehman College
The City University of New York

Franklin Watts
New York | London | Toronto | 1979

Cartoons courtesy of ROTHCO: p. 6 (Liederman–
Long Island Press, New York); p. 18 (Audley-
London Sunday Telegraph); p. 32 (Konopacki);
p. 39 (Troop); p. 48 (Pat Fink); p. 51 (Punch);
p. 56 (Liederman–Long Island Press, New York);
p. 61 (Padry–Le Herisson, Paris); p. 66 (Bender–
Waterloo Courier, Iowa); p. 77 (Renault–Sacra-
mento Bee, California); p. 84 (Pierotti); p. 91
(Hilton).

Library of Congress Cataloging in Publication Data
Radding, Charles.
    The modern presidency.

    (American Government series)
    Bibliography: p.
    Includes index.
    SUMMARY: Discusses the Presidency, includ-
ing the responsibilities of the President, the exer-
sise and restraint of Presidential power, and the
election of the chief executive.
    1. Presidents—United States—Juvenile lit-
erature. [1. Presidents] I. Title.
JK517.R3   353.03'13   79–12469
ISBN 0–531–02266–8

CONTENTS

The Modern
Presidency

CHAPTER ONE

The Presidency
and the Constitution

The Articles of Confederation, as the first constitution of the United States was called, had been drawn up during the Revolution. At that time, the states had just declared their independence from Britain, and the people—fearful of installing a tyrannical government like the one they had just broken free from—had not been willing to give up many of their powers to the new central government. Therefore, the national government under the Articles was quite weak. It could not raise an army or impose taxes. It could not regulate trade, either within the United States or with foreign countries. It could not pass laws binding on U.S. citizens.

In time, though, the need for a stronger central government became apparent. The system just was not functioning efficiently. Congress, being the only branch of the national government, was forced to handle an inordinate amount of business. During the Revolutionary War, for example, members of Congress who had many pressing duties had to find time to serve on committees to buy gunpowder for the Army or outfit armed ships. If the members of the committees could not agree, the entire Congress often had to meet to settle the dispute. The use of committees to handle day to day administration worked so badly that by the 1780s Congress itself started to turn over many of these responsibilities to outside officials.

There were other reasons, too, for wanting a stronger central government. In the 1780s, many state governments were suffering from great instability. Laws were being repealed or altered so frequently that it was difficult for ordinary people to know what the law was. Many state legislatures were passing laws favoring one part of society at the expense of another. This led to bitter struggles for government control between groups within the states, and in some cases these struggles led to outright rebellion. In 1786, for example, farmers in western Massachusetts, led by Daniel Shay, defied the state government, which was based in Boston. Shay's group had to be suppressed by military force. In Virginia, in 1787, some groups set fire to their local courthouses and prevented the collection of state taxes they felt were unfair. The Federalists, as those who wanted a stronger central government were called, believed that the bitter struggles to control the state governments would cease if some of the states' powers were transferred to the federal government.

THE CONSTITUTION'S SOLUTION: CONGRESS VERSUS THE PRESIDENCY

The Constitutional Convention met in the summer of 1787 with the announced purpose of revising the Articles of Confederation and finding ways to strengthen the national government. The members of the Convention could have accomplished their mission without creating a strong President. They could have done so simply by giving more power to Congress, the power to tax, for example, or to regulate commerce. Congress itself could have been given the right to appoint officials to carry out its policies, much as the British Parliament of today appoints a Prime Minister. This kind of government would have had the advantage of remaining closely bound to the desires of its citizens.

In fact, the members of the Convention had good reason to fear giving too much power to an independent executive. They remembered how, as colonists, they had suffered under the strong executive hand of the British monarchy and its corrupt appointed officials. They did not want a President who might end up replacing the king they had so recently overthrown.

The members of the Convention were also well aware, however, of the dangers that could exist under a congressional government. As the Convention members themselves had seen occurring in state governments, majorities sometimes totally disregarded the interests of the minorities. There could result a legislative tyranny, a tyranny of the majority instead of a tyranny by a king or executive. James Madison was thinking about just this when he wrote to Thomas Jefferson in April 1787, shortly before the Constitutional Convention met: "Wherever the real power in a Government lies, there is danger of oppression. In our government the real power lies in the majority of the Community, and the invasion of private rights is chiefly to be apprehended, not from acts of Government contrary to the sense of its constituents, but from acts in which the Government is the mere instrument of the major number of the constituents."

The members of the Constitutional Convention were faced, therefore, with a great challenge. They wanted a strong central government, but they did not want to place in jeopardy the freedom they had won in the Revolution. As Madison later put it, "[We] must first enable the government to control the governed; and in the next place oblige it to control itself."

The Constitution represents a bold solution to this challenge. It gives great power to the central government, but it divides that power between a strong President and a strong Congress. Neither one can act for long without the cooperation of the other. In foreign relations, for example, Presidents receive foreign ambassadors and appoint U.S. ambassadors to foreign countries with the approval of the Senate. Presidents can negotiate on behalf of the United States with governments of foreign countries, but the Senate must ratify by a two-thirds vote any treaties made by a President. These arrangements were intended to permit Presidents to conduct diplomatic negotiations in secret but to prevent them from making promises to foreign countries that the people of the United States might not approve of.

These provisions, which are called checks and balances, affect almost every power the Constitution gives to the Presidency. Not that they were intended to be invoked only when there was danger of tyranny. On the contrary, the framers of the Constitution expected that there would be frequent conflicts between the branches of government, and they counted on these conflicts to keep the government of the United States from violating the liberties of Americans. They felt safe in creating a strong Presidency because they had also created a strong Congress. They expected that senators and representatives would be proud of their responsibilities and insist on frank discussion

and careful scrutiny of all presidential proposals. They also expected that the members of Congress would have an interest in local issues that a President might ignore, and they counted on Congress to weigh local interests against national interests. Finally, they counted on judges nominated by the President and confirmed by the Senate to punish politicians who tried to ignore the laws. In sum, the framers expected rivalry between the branches of the central government to continue and thus to prevent the central government itself from becoming too powerful.

We can get a good idea of how the framers envisioned the Presidency by looking closely at the checks and balances that apply to the President's most important areas of responsibility: execution of the laws, enactment of legislation, appointment of judges, command of the armed forces, and relations with foreign countries. In each of these areas the President is given responsibility for gathering information and carrying out policies, but Congress has ultimate responsibility for deciding or approving policies before they go into effect. In addition, because of its impeachment powers, Congress is also the final judge of any President.

CONSTITUTIONAL RESTRICTIONS ON THE POWER OF THE PRESIDENCY

The Constitution vests the executive power of the United States in the President and says that the President "shall take Care that the Laws be faithfully executed" (Article II, Section 3). This means not only that Presidents must arrest criminals who violate federal law, but they must also see to it that all the activities of the federal government are carried out efficiently and as Congress intended, whether that activity be road construction, collection of taxes and tariffs, purchase of weapons, payment of salaries of U.S. employees, or the like. The framers believed that enforcing the laws should be the unique responsibility of the executive branch, and they gave the office of the Presidency enough power to enable this task to be carried out effectively. Presidents, for example, with the consent of the Senate, appoint the highest officers of the federal government. If an office becomes vacant while the Senate is not in session, the President can name someone to fill it at least until the Senate reconvenes and is able to review the appointment. The President can ask officers of the executive branch for their opinion on questions of national policy and can dismiss any officials whose work is not judged satisfactory.

The framers did not give these powers to the Presidency simply because they wanted a strong chief executive. One of the main reasons they decided that a President, and not a committee, should be in charge of the executive branch was so that there would be some one person to take ultimate responsibility for stupid or crooked acts committed by the executive branch. They planned it so that the President, who could appoint and remove officials, would also be subject to impeachment for failing to run the executive branch properly. In this way, the framers were able to give the President power without destroying Congress's right and duty to remove a President who fails to carry out the laws.

The President was given certain legislative duties too. Presidents are supposed to keep Congress informed of the "state of the Union" and should recommend new laws to Congress when they believe them to be necessary. Presidents can also call special sessions of Congress to deal with emergencies, can veto bills passed by Congress, and, if

Congress adjourns soon after passing a bill, can use a "pocket veto" by refusing to sign the bill.

However, a President's veto power is not absolute. Legislation becomes law if the President fails to sign or veto it and Congress remains in session for at least ten days after the bill is passed. Moreover, Congress can enact a law over the President's veto by a two-thirds vote in each house. Congress can also force a President to accept legislation he or she does not want by including it in a bill with legislation the President does want, because the Constitution gives the President the power to accept or reject bills *only* in the form that Congress passes them.

Judges are appointed by the President in the same way that other U.S. officials are appointed, by Senate confirmation of a presidential nomination. However, unlike members of the executive branch, judges are not the subordinates of the President. The President cannot give them instructions nor remove them from office, and they do not need to have the confidence of the President in order to do their job. Instead, judges are expected to act independently of both the President and Congress and to restrain unconstitutional action no matter who commits it. For this reason, the Senate usually gives judicial nominations more careful scrutiny than other executive nominations and is more willing to reject one it considers unqualified.

The Constitution carefully divides the responsibility for national defense, which includes the power to declare and fight wars, between the President and Congress. The President is the Commander in Chief of the U.S. Armed Forces. When the country is at war, the President selects commanders for the Armed Forces and oversees military operations. However, the Armed Forces can be recruited and paid for only by acts of Congress and war can be declared only by Congress. This last provision, that Congress should decide when to go to war, is particularly significant because it reveals the unwillingness of the framers to let Presidents make this crucial decision. The framers knew from their own experience that executives often begin wars out of pride, foolishness, desire for glory, or other personal reasons, and they did not want Americans to suffer and die needlessly. They felt that the United States should engage in such a serious and costly undertaking as war only after a full and open debate. As Madison explained in a letter to Jefferson: "The Constitution supposes . . . that the Executive is the branch of power most interested in war and most prone to it. It has accordingly with studied care vested the question of war in the Legislative."

INSTALLING THE ELECTORAL COLLEGE

Concern about separation of powers also influenced the Convention's debate over how the President should be chosen. Some delegates wanted Congress to elect the President. This proposal was opposed by other delegates who were afraid that a President chosen by Congress would be reluctant to oppose Congress later. Another suggestion was to have the President elected by popular vote. This would give the President an independent base of support. However, some delegates doubted that ordinary people were in a position to judge who was best qualified for the job. They saw the President's job as basically an administrative one. It would be the President's duty to carry out the laws passed by Congress. Some delegates feared that the person elected President by the common people would be a clever politician but not necessarily an effective administrator.

The electoral college was finally accepted as a compromise between these positions. Each state was to cast as many votes in the electoral college as it had members in the House of Representatives and the Senate combined. The person who received a majority of the electoral votes would become President, and the person who received the next largest number would become Vice-President. The electors themselves would be voted in by their communities and were expected by the founding fathers to be prominent citizens. Thus they could be counted on more than the average person to make a wise choice in their selection of a President.

The founding fathers thought that there would be many occasions when no single person received a majority of the electoral votes. For this reason, they provided for the House of Representatives to choose the President from among the five candidates with the largest number of electoral votes.

THE POPULAR PRESIDENCY

At the time the Constitution was ratified, Madison and others expected Congress to be the dominant branch of government because the members of Congress were elected directly by the people. This situation was altered, however, by the growth of political parties. Choosing a President became a political, partisan issue, and electors were chosen on the basis of the candidate they supported and not on their own merit. The winner of the election, therefore, was able to claim a popular mandate—the support of the common people—and could act independently of Congress as long as he or she retained strong popular support. Thus, the nature of the office of the Presidency changed. Congress did not dare impeach a popular President. On the other hand, Presidents who lacked popular support found their independence severely limited.

In the nineteenth century, the ability of the President to influence popular opinion and gather support was still limited by the slowness of communications. Even during election campaigns, candidates often stayed home and let their party organizations do the work of winning votes. Consequently, few people ever saw the President. The invention of the telegraph, although it permitted news to travel much faster, still did not bring the President into direct contact with the electorate. In the twentieth century, however, radio and television have brought the Presidency much closer to the public. Journalists covered the activities of Presidents and their families in great detail, and voters often knew more about the Presidents than about their own senators and representatives. Beginning with Franklin D. Roosevelt, Presidents have used radio and television to put their views on political issues directly before the public. These presidential efforts at persuasion have not always been successful, but the ability of Presidents to dominate the news has made it harder for other politicians to get their opinions heard.

The Presidency has also gained strength in the twentieth century because of the growing importance of the U.S. role in world affairs. World War I was the first major U.S. involvement in a European struggle, and the U.S. became fully committed to a world role during World War II. During the Cold War with the Soviet Union that followed World War II, most Americans believed that national security required speed and secrecy in government.

Voters assessed presidential candidates more on their abilities to manage foreign policy and less on their domestic policies, and Presidents began to act independently of the slower, more public Congress. National security also became an excuse for preventing Congress and the public from examining much of the routine business of the executive branch. This trend was brought to light in the early 1970s by revelations concerning the Vietnam War and the Watergate Affair. For the first time in quite a while, the dangers of concentrating too much power in the hands of the President were revealed. But the Presidency still remains much stronger than it was before World War II.

The Presidency, therefore, has changed a great deal since the Constitution was written. In the following chapters we will examine the modern Presidency to see how it works under the Constitution today and how it has evolved from the original conception of the founding fathers.

CHAPTER TWO

Electing the President

THE ELECTORAL COLLEGE

Legally the electoral college, established at the Constitutional Convention and reformed by the Twelfth Amendment to the Constitution, is still the way we select our Presidents. In the November election in a presidential year, voters in every state choose electors. In December the electors from each state cast their votes for President. In January these votes are counted by Congress and the new President is officially named. However, the members of the electoral college no longer really elect the President. They are simply agents of the voters of each state. In most states the names of the electors do not even appear on the November ballot; voters simply indicate the party or candidate whose electors they want. The men or women who run as electors are chosen by their state's party or its campaign committee, and they must pledge to vote for their party's candidate if they become electors.

Still, the electoral college is not just a harmless anachronism. There are many ways in which it continues to influence American government. First, the way electoral votes are apportioned among the states gives greater weight to the votes of states with small populations than to those with large populations. Under the Constitution, each state casts an electoral vote for every member of its congressional delegation, senator or representative. Vermont, for example, which has one representative, casts three electoral votes; New York, which has thirty-nine representatives, casts forty-one electoral votes. Since there are about forty times as many New Yorkers as there are Vermonters, this arrangement means that the individual Vermonter has almost three times as much influence in the electoral college as the individual New Yorker.

The electoral college also tends to discourage voter participation in politics in states where one political party has an overwhelming majority. Since a plurality of one vote in a state's popular vote is enough to award all the state's electoral votes to a candidate, voters can easily come to feel that their own vote won't make any difference. A Republican in a heavily Democratic state such as Massachusetts may be discouraged from voting because even before the election he or she can be reasonably certain Massachusetts will go Democratic. The Massachusetts Republican knows his or her vote won't count, even though the national election may be very close. Similarly, a member of a majority party may not feel his or her vote is needed, since victory at the state level—the only level that counts in the electoral college—is already assured. In this way, the

"We get this one for understanding how
the democratic nomination system works."

electoral college can make average voters feel their votes are not important.

It is also possible for electors to run as "unpledged." In these cases the electors are committed to no particular candidate within a party. This situation occurred in some Southern states in the 1960s. The unpledged electors had hoped to bargain with the candidates for concessions in the area of civil rights if there was a close election. It has also sometimes happened that electors broke their pledge to vote for a particular candidate and voted for someone else. This has never changed the outcome of an election, but it does emphasize what could happen.

Finally, and most important, the electoral college makes it possible for the candidate who receives the greatest number of popular votes in an election to be defeated by another candidate who receives fewer votes but wins a majority in the electoral college. This can occur because all of a state's electoral votes are cast for whoever gets the most popular votes in that state. If Peter Jones gets one thousand more votes in New York than Mary Smith, he gets all of New York's electoral votes. Smith, meanwhile, may have beaten Jones in Vermont by two thousand votes. When the popular votes of New York and Vermont are added together, Smith has one thousand more votes, but Jones has many more electoral votes. If the same proportions were true in the other states, Jones would be the President, even though more people voted for Smith.

Something like this actually happened in 1888, when Benjamin Harrison lost to Grover Cleveland in the popular vote but became President through the electoral college. It nearly happened again in 1976, when Jimmy Carter ran against Gerald Ford. On election night, it became obvious early in the evening that Carter was going to receive a majority of the popular vote. However, because the totals for each candidate were very close in several states, it seemed possible for several hours that Ford might actually win a majority of the electoral vote. When the final returns were counted, it was discovered that a change of 9,245 votes in Ohio and 3,687 in Hawaii would have given the election to Ford, although Carter would have retained a majority of 1.7 million votes in the nationwide popular totals.

Perhaps because of this close call, reform of the electoral college has again become a political issue. One suggestion that has received a great deal of support is an amendment that would award the Presidency to the candidate with the greatest overall popular vote, as long as that candidate received at least 40 percent of the votes cast. If no candidate received 40 percent of the popular votes, then the President would be chosen from among the candidates by a joint session of Congress, each member of Congress casting one vote.

Despite the advantages of direct election of the President, the electoral college still has substantial support. Residents of states such as Alaska and Delaware are afraid that presidential candidates would never come to their states were it not for the disproportionate weight they pull in the electoral college. Similarly, voting coalitions in some large states would lose influence.

Another reason given for retaining the electoral college is that it supports a two-party system in the United States. Major parties have an advantage under the electoral college, because voters who might prefer a third-party candidate often end up voting for a Republican or Democrat so that they can influence how their state's electoral votes are cast. In 1976, for example, Eugene McCarthy had trouble getting support for his independent candidacy for President because he was not able to get on the ballot in enough states to have a chance of winning in the electoral college. Many voters who liked McCarthy seem to have decided to choose between Ford and Carter so that their votes would not be wasted. A system of direct election of the President might not compel voters to make that choice. On the other hand, it could also be argued that by forcing voters to choose between two major-party candidates, the electoral college deprives voters of the opportunity to express their real preferences for President, with the result that sometimes Presidents are elected whom nobody feels very enthusiastic about.

In sum, then, the electoral college is supported by those who are afraid that abandoning it will deprive them of influence, or will at least have unforeseeable damaging effects on American politics. Supporters of direct election of the President argue that the foreseeable dangers of maintaining the electoral college are at least as bad as anything that could result from a change, and that direct election of the President would encourage fuller participation of the electorate in national elections.

PLANNING THE EARLY STAGES
OF THE CAMPAIGN

In practice, of course, the election of the President begins long before the electors cast their votes. Because of the importance of the two-party system in American politics—and we have seen how the electoral college contributes to this—anyone who wants to be President usually has to win the nomination of the Republican or Democratic party. Sometimes one person—usually a President or a

Vice-President—has so much support from his or her party that no one else tries to win the nomination. In these cases, primaries and even the nominating convention are mostly formalities. More often, however, there are several candidates for President, and their campaigns may begin years before the nominating convention.

An aspiring presidential candidate usually begins by preparing a strategy for the campaign. This strategy includes determining what kind of image the candidate will want to project, which states will be most important to his or her chances of winning the nomination, and which opponents to expect to receive challenges from. For example, Jimmy Carter's planning for his campaign for President began in 1972 with a memo from an adviser on how to project the image of a nationally important politician. The adviser urged Carter first to publicize his accomplishments as governor of Georgia, next to make it appear he was a leader of the Democratic party, and only then to reveal his ambitions as a possible presidential candidate. Another early memo of the Carter campaign selected certain states as important to Carter's success: New Hampshire and Florida, because their primaries were held early in the campaign, and Pennsylvania and Ohio, because they were industrial and traditionally Democratic states. This second memo also urged Carter to develop expertise in foreign affairs by travel abroad and to write a book—both of which Carter did in preparation for his campaign.

Presidential campaigns are not, however, based entirely on preparing and then publicizing an image of the candidate, nor on the drafting of an effective campaign plan. To be successful, a candidate needs the help of many people across the country, people who are willing to spend a great deal of time organizing local campaigns. Since no candidate has enough money to simply hire all the workers he or she needs, the recruitment of volunteers is always a major objective in the early stages of a campaign.

There are many different ways in which volunteer organizations are built up. Politicians with established national reputations—particularly those who have run for national office before—can often rely on old friends and supporters from previous campaigns. In 1972, for example, Hubert Humphrey had little trouble establishing his campaign organization because of the contacts he had developed as Vice-President and as a candidate for President earlier, in 1960 and 1968. Even in 1976, when Humphrey was not a declared candidate, these old associates could have formed the basis for a campaign if Humphrey had changed his mind and decided to run.

Politicians without such experience and reputations have to work harder to build up their campaign organizations. Carter, for example, used his position as chairman of the 1974 Democratic National Campaign Committee to travel around the country and make friends. Throughout his travels, a Carter aide carefully took down the names and addresses of the people he spoke with so that they could be contacted later. In New York, Carter met Midge Costanza, who was trying to unseat a Republican congressman. Costanza later cochaired Carter's New York State campaign. While in California, Carter spoke to a group of environmentalists, one of whom later became a cochairman of his California campaign.

In addition to building campaign organizations, presidential hopefuls also spend a great deal of time in the preelection years raising money. Presidential campaigns are expensive, even before the active campaigning for delegates begins. Candidates must be able to pay the salaries of their professional staff and to cover the costs of travel, telephones, and office space. In addition, they must build up sufficient cash reserves to meet the expenses of the early primaries, such as are incurred in the printing of campaign literature and the buying of advertising time on radio and television.

For all of these reasons, raising money has always been a major part of any presidential campaign. But it has become even more important since the enactment of the national campaign financing law, which was itself inspired by the Watergate revelations. Formerly, candidates were often forced to take large amounts of money from wealthy supporters; just a few of these "fat cats" could entirely finance the early stages of a presidential campaign. But then, of course, the candidates would be in the position of owing the fat cats favors in return. Under the new law, any candidate can qualify for federal subsidies by raising $5,000 in each of twenty states, but he or she must do this in amounts of $250 or less. To obtain the subsidies, the candidate must also promise not to accept contributions of more than $1,000 from anyone. Since at least one thousand contributors are needed to raise $1,000,000, the new law favors those candidates who have won fairly extensive popular support already.

Sometimes candidates will abandon the presidential race even before the beginning of an election year. There are many reasons for this. They may find that the campaigning takes them away from their families too much of the time. This is unfortunate, because although most Americans consider family life important, the length of the campaign favors candidates who are willing to give it up. Candidates may also find they are having trouble raising money under the new campaign law, or that they cannot seem to generate much interest among voters. Women and minority candidates are particularly likely to suffer from this—as Catholics did before John Kennedy showed a Catholic could be elected President—because few people take seriously their chances of winning. As popular attitudes change, however, women and minority candidates will experience fewer problems of winning support for their candidacies.

At the beginning of an election year, those who do remain candidates must turn their attention to winning delegates. This is a complicated and time-consuming process. State parties choose delegates in many different ways, and the selection process continues throughout the winter and spring. Some states have statewide primaries in which voters choose specific delegates who are either pledged to their favorite candidate or, sometimes, not pledged to anyone. Other states have primaries in which the state's convention delegation is apportioned among the candidates according to the share of the primary vote each candidate receives. Still other states choose delegates during conventions attended by representatives of county or precinct parties.

To be successful, candidates must be able to appeal to voters whom they meet personally and to attract favorable news coverage. Campaign trips are important during this period, as much for the publicity they create as for the number of voters the candidates actually meet. Campaign managers try to create events that will attract press coverage. In 1976, for example, one candidate, former Senator Fred Harris of Oklahoma, traveled around the country in a camper to demonstrate that he was running an economical, populist campaign and really wanted to meet the people. Candidates on tour also try to appear on local news or interview broadcasts, where they can be seen without having had to spend any money. The money that is allocated for advertising, moreover, must be spent well. Not only do commercials need to present an appealing image of the candidate, but they must be broadcast at the right times and on the right radio and television stations to reach the most voters possible for the money spent. Candidates who fail to plan their expenditures efficiently often find that they have run out of money even before they reach states where a little extra advertising would do a lot of good. In 1976, for example, Senator Henry Jackson exhausted almost all of his funds before the Pennsylvania primary, where lack of advertising contributed to his decisive loss to Jimmy Carter.

In addition to attracting as much favorable attention as possible, candidates must see that their local organizations are providing effective support for their bid. The volunteer supporters in each state won by the candidate in the pre-election years become the nucleus of a much larger organization as the time for choosing delegates approaches. Workers must be recruited to carry the candidate's message from door to door, to make telephone calls, and to make sure voters favorable to the candidate actually vote on primary day. In the 1976 Massachusetts primary, for example, Senator Jackson's organization hired five hundred automobiles and drivers to take voters to the polls. This effort undoubtedly contributed to Jackson's victory in that primary. Projects such as these can be organized by members of the paid national staff, but since only one or two professionals are put in charge of each state, most of the planning and actual work must be done by recruited volunteers.

Shortly after the selection of delegates begins, many candidates drop out of the race—the ones who are not making a good early showing. Since they have won little support from voters and appear to have little chance of winning, these candidates find it harder and harder to recruit volunteers and to obtain the money they need for travel, staff salaries, and advertising. Further, the press generally starts to pay them less attention as it begins to concentrate on the front-runners.

The 1976 campaign illustrates this well. In 1976 Fred Harris, former vice-presidential candidate Sargent Shriver, and Senator Birch Bayh were all knocked out of the race after weak showings in the first few primaries. Carter, meanwhile, had shown strength in Iowa caucuses and the New Hampshire primary, and in Florida early in March he defeated Alabama governor George Wallace and Senator Jackson. The Florida victory was especially important because it showed politicians Carter could win in the South even though he was much more moderate on issues of race relations than Wallace. Carter finished off Wallace's candidacy by winning in Illinois and North Carolina, where Wallace had previously shown strength, and Jackson withdrew from active campaigning after losing in Pennsylvania. Carter's victory in Pennsylvania was significant because it showed he could defeat Jackson even where Jackson had strong support from organized labor, which has always played an important role in Democratic party politics. By the beginning of May, Carter faced only Representative Morris Udall of all the candidates who had been active at the beginning of the year, and a stop-Carter movement was beginning to form.

The later primaries of May and June are usually crucial to the success of presidential campaigns. If the race has narrowed to two candidates, these primaries offer each the chance to win enough delegates to secure the nomination. In May 1976, former Governor Ronald Reagan of California and President Gerald Ford were the only viable Republican candidates running, as they had been for the whole primary season. Reagan had already proven his attractiveness to Republican voters in earlier primaries, so he had to be taken seriously as a challenger to Ford, and his supporters were enthusiastic about his chances. The May and June primaries, therefore, became particularly sharply contested.

A different situation usually develops if a single candidate emerges by May as the leader in convention delegates. In this case, there is often an attempt by politicians opposing that candidate to form coalitions to block a first-ballot victory at the convention. The Democratic contest of 1976 provides a good example of this. After Carter had eliminated most of his early rivals, some Carter opponents tried to enlist former Vice-President Hubert Humphrey, a popular figure in the party, to run as a "compromise" candidate. Humphrey refused, but Senator Frank Church of Idaho and Governor Edmund Brown, Jr., of California announced as candidates, and each scored primary victories against Carter. Other politicians tried to run slates of "uncommitted" delegates as an alternative to Carter. This ABC movement (Anybody But Carter) is not at all unique; a similar effort had been directed against George McGovern in 1972 and in the Republican party against Nixon in 1968, though all these movements ultimately failed.

Between the election of the last primary candidates and the beginning of the nominating convention, there are usually several weeks when candidates can test their strength and try to win support from uncommitted delegates, perhaps by citing public opinion polls that show they have the best chance to win in the general election. Political activity in this period usually involves a struggle to shape the party platform so that it reflects the views of one candidate or another. Candidates also clash over procedural issues such as convention rules or which delegates to seat when there are disputes about who represents certain states. These issues can have great influence on the course of the convention itself.

At this time, a great deal of attention is also given to political leaders of states that have large numbers of delegates still not truly committed. There may be one or more states that have a local party running as a favorite son candidate. Or, the local party organization of a state may be running an uncommitted slate of delegates. Either way, it is not unusual for there to be several blocs of delegate votes at the convention which will go as the local "boss" desires. This makes the bosses important figures at the convention, and sometimes their influence is so great that it makes them nationally important even between presidential elections. In the 1960s and 1970s Mayor Richard Daley of Chicago was a boss of this kind. After Carter won substantial victories on the last day of the primaries in 1976, Daley threw his support and delegates to Carter. These delegates assured Carter's nomination.

AT THE CONVENTION

The actual balloting for President usually takes place on the second or third day of the convention, after the approval of the party platform. In recent years, the nominees have been chosen on the first ballot because one of the candidates had already amassed a majority of the delegates before the convention began. Previous conventions had required several ballots to choose a nominee. In these situations, leaders of various groups were forced to compromise in their selection of presidential and vice-presidential nominees. Because the final choice was someone who was finally acceptable to so many different groups, it rarely occurred that the candidates who led in the early ballots were chosen.

Following the selection of the presidential nominee is the selection of the vice-presidential nominee. If there was a compromise, the vice-presidential spot goes to someone agreed on in the compromise package. Otherwise, the presidential nominee makes the selection. Vice-presidential candidates are usually selected because they balance the ticket in some way—for example by coming from a different region than the presidential candidate, by being more liberal or more conservative, or by being members of a different ethnic, religious, or social group. The selection of the vice-presidential nominee has to be done in a hurry, and this sometimes leads to problems, as it did in 1972 when the Democratic vice-presidential nominee, Senator Thomas Eagleton, was forced to withdraw when it became public knowledge that he had had past problems with mental health.

THE GENERAL ELECTION CAMPAIGN

The actual election campaign traditionally begins around Labor Day and requires many of the same efforts as the primaries: organizing campaign strategy, appealing to voters both in person and through advertisements, and so on. The fall campaign is, of course, much more complicated, simply because it is much bigger. Money must be spent in many of the fifty states at once, and apportioned among the states according to a national strategy. Candidates can spend only a few days or hours in each locality, and running of state campaign organizations must be left to local politicians, since the candidate's personal staff is too small to accomplish everything. However, the greatest difference between the primaries and the national campaign is in the nature of the electorate. In the primaries, the candidate seeks only the votes of members of his or her own party, and usually only people interested in politics bother to vote. In the fall, the party nominees have to win the votes of many people who are largely indifferent to politics and of people who do not share political affiliations.

One consequence of adjusting to the demands of the fall campaign is that candidates often compromise their positions on issues. A statement that appeals to one party's members may not be as effective with independent voters or with members of the opposite party. New issues arise that were not important during the primaries because the candidates were from the same parties. Republicans may have to defend themselves against charges they are indifferent to unemployment or to social injustice, issues that are rarely raised in Republican primaries. Democrats, on the other hand, may have to argue that they are not big spenders or that they will not create large budget deficits, raise taxes, or push for inflationary programs. Another important difference in the fall campaign is the greater reliance on the news media to get the candidate's message

"It's the issueless candidate!!"

across to voters. Often, candidates concentrate more on how to convey an appealing image of themselves than on communicating how they will deal with issues. Incumbent Presidents, for example, usually try to seem "presidential" and stress their experience in office. Often they spend a great deal of time during this period in the White House, where they can get frequent news coverage as they go through their daily routines and be seen as too important to the government to be able to leave Washington. Youthful or relatively unknown candidates, such as Jimmy Carter in 1976, may try to point out that they had no share in the mistakes of previous years and promise to "get the country moving again."

The close attention given both major-party candidates in the news media at this time sometimes has the effect of overemphasizing relatively trivial issues that lend themselves to easy coverage in daily papers or on evening news broadcasts. In 1976, for example, President Ford described Eastern European countries as free from Soviet domination on one of the televised debates between the candidates. Whatever Ford had in mind when he said that, the fact is that he had never in his entire political career shown any lack of sensitivity concerning countries subject to Soviet rule. His statement, however, was made an issue by news reporters and Democrats, and Ford spent nearly two weeks of the campaign trying to explain his statement.

Many of the 60 percent of eligible voters who actually vote on Election Day cast their ballots on the basis of images the media projects. This situation is often criticized because images can be false. What is more serious, though, is that the nature of the campaign favors nominees who can give quick, appealing answers to questions over those who are more deliberate or more reluctant to make snap judgments. Many Presidents carry the habit of quick response over into the White House, where relatively few policy issues require such spur-of-the-moment reactions. Nominees are also sometimes able to avoid altogether stating their positions on issues, and when elected adopt policies that differ in many ways from what they hinted they believed in. Unfortunately, there is no solution to this problem until voters refuse to vote for candidates who do not state their opinions clearly and honestly and their reasons for thinking as they do.

CHAPTER THREE

The Responsibilities of the President

The modern Presidency can be most easily understood in terms of the different jobs the President does. Five of these jobs are particularly important: chief of state, chief executive, commander in chief of the Armed Forces, maker of foreign policy, and party leader. All except the role of party leader were provided for by the Constitution, but the actual responsibilities of these jobs have changed a great deal since the Constitution was written.

CHIEF OF STATE

When political scientists say the President is chief of state of the United States, they mean that he or she represents the people of the United States and the U.S. government at formal ceremonies and at informal gatherings. The President receives foreign diplomats, welcomes visiting chiefs of state, lights the national Christmas tree on the

White House lawn, issues the Thanksgiving Day message, honors the Tomb of the Unknown Soldier, throws out the first baseball of the major-league season, attends the Army–Navy football game—and the list could go on and on. At all these events, the President functions as a symbol of the nation and spokesman for its people.

One major problem with the President's assuming this symbolic role is that it is all too easy for voters to confuse the symbolic leader with the individual politician who holds the office. This kind of confusion does not occur in every country, because many nations have chiefs of state who have no practical political power. In Britain, for example, the ruling monarch is chief of state and performs all ceremonial and symbolic duties. The monarch does not, however, make decisions concerning the daily operation of the government. That job is left to the Prime Minister. In other countries, such as West Germany, there are elected symbolic Presidents, with political power again left in the hands of a Prime Minister. This kind of arrangement makes it easy for citizens to demonstrate respect for the chief of state as a symbol of their country even when they disagree with the policies followed by the government in power.

The double role of the President under the American system has often led to controversy. In the late 1960s and early 1970s, for example, citizens who opposed President Johnson's and President Nixon's policies in Vietnam sometimes showed their feelings by picketing or heckling whenever these Presidents made public appearances. Some Americans were shocked by these demonstrations; they felt the protesters were showing disrespect for their country. President Nixon often played on these feelings by denouncing the protesters—who were merely exercising their right to disagree on a political issue.

The desire to have a President who would make a good symbol for the nation can also affect the way voters vote in presidential elections. Many nineteenth-century Presidents were generals who had little or no previous political experience. Andrew Jackson, Zachary Taylor, William Henry Harrison, and Ulysses S. Grant were all elected after successful military careers, and of them all, only Jackson proved a particularly able President. In the 1952 and 1956 presidential elections Dwight D. Eisenhower, a war hero and a genial and distinguished-looking man, had a considerable advantage over Adlai Stevenson because Eisenhower was perceived as looking more like a President. Many observers believe that Richard Nixon lost to John Kennedy in the election of 1960 because Nixon's makeup at one of the televised debates between the two made him appear as though he had a sinister shadow of a beard.

But perhaps the most striking effect of having a President also be the symbolic head of state is seen when an incumbent President runs for re-election. As the incumbent, the President flies around the country in *Air Force One*, the President's private plane. Each appearance of the President is marked by the playing of "Hail to the Chief," the presidential anthem. The President travels surrounded by bodyguards, and the presidential seal is used to decorate the podium even at campaign rallies. Often, incumbents will do their best to merge their own identity with that of the national symbol. President Nixon, for example, was rarely even referred to by name in 1972; his campaign committee was called the Committee to Re-Elect the President, and many posters and stickers simply said "Re-Elect the President." Similarly, in 1976 Gerald Ford re-

**"Politicians make the mistake of forgetting
that they've been *appointed*, not *anointed*!"**

mained in the White House during several of the early weeks of the campaign just to emphasize his incumbency. His main public appearances were to sign bills in the White House Rose Garden, and he purposefully began to wear a distinguished-looking vest with his suit. By these means he encouraged people to think about him as a symbol instead of as a politician.

The ceremonial aspects of the Presidency are, therefore, more than merely a drain on the President's time. They make it harder for political opponents to criticize presidential policies. They help to emphasize the role of "image" in national politics. And they make it easier for a President to gain re-election.

CHIEF EXECUTIVE

The framers of the Constitution believed that the President's main responsibility would be to enforce the laws. This job has grown enormously since the Constitution was written. Today, the President supervises an executive branch that employs over three million people and accounts for almost all the billions of dollars spent by the federal government. All the Cabinet-level departments of government—such as State; Defense; and Health, Education, and Welfare—belong to the executive branch, as do many independent agencies, such as the Central Intelligence Agency (CIA). In addition, the personal staff of the President has itself grown considerably in recent years. However, despite the size of the executive branch, the President still remains constitutionally responsible for all of its actions, just as in the eighteenth century, and except for the Vice-President, the President is still the only elected executive officer.

When we hear the words "enforce the laws," the phrase which the Constitution uses to describe the President's job, we naturally think of arresting criminals. This is, to be sure, one task of the Department of Justice, which as part of the executive branch is under the President. But sometimes the laws which need enforcement are not the ones we ordinarily think of as laws. For example in 1954 the Supreme Court declared that the segregation of public schools according to race was unconstitutional. In accord with this, the federal Court of Appeals approved in 1957 a plan by the Little Rock, Arkansas, Board of Education to integrate Little Rock's schools, beginning with Central High School. When it came time for the plan to be put into effect, however, Orval Faubus, the governor of Arkansas, ordered the National Guard to surround the school and prevent the black children from attending. The local federal district court ordered Governor Faubus to cease his obstruction of integration, but when the troops were withdrawn, a crowd of angry citizens formed, determined to keep the blacks out themselves. To deal with this crisis, and to carry out the law as interpreted by the courts, President Eisenhower decided to send regular U.S. Army troops to Little Rock to restore order.

This was a dramatic instance of a President's acting to enforce the laws, but most cases are quite different. Usually, there is no question of forcing people to comply with a law they wish to resist; more often, the executive must merely be the one to decide how legislation enacted by Congress is to be carried out. Thus, when Congress decides to purchase a new plane for the Air Force or a new ship for the Navy, it is the executive branch that draws up the specifications, takes bids from contractors, awards the contract, and oversees the successful completion of the project. When a new federal road is to be built, the route is laid out and standards of quality are set up by the executive branch. When laws controlling water or air pollution are passed by Congress, it is the executive branch that enforces the standards and decides when exceptions to the laws should be permitted. Even the payment of social security benefits is carried out by the executive branch of the government, which sets up the rules and enforces them. In all these ways, and many more, the executive branch under the President influences the lives of every citizen.

Presidents can also use their executive powers to shape government policy on controversial issues. An early example of this was the struggle of Andrew Jackson against the Second Bank of the United States. The Bank was not a public institution; it was a private corporation chartered by the Congress and exempt from state taxes. In return for its exemption from taxation, the Bank handled U.S. government deposits without charge. But Jackson disagreed with the Bank's monetary policies, and in 1832 he vetoed a bill of Congress that would have extended the Bank's charter, which was due to expire in 1836. Jackson feared that the Bank might still use its financial power against him, however, and in 1833 he withdrew all government deposits from it. This use of executive power assured Jackson control of government policy despite the opposition of Congress.

A further example of how important these matters can be concerns another case of discrimination. In response to increasing demands for racial equality in the late 1940s, President Truman abolished racial discrimination in the Armed Forces simply by telling the Armed Forces that there were to be no more segregated units. No act of Congress was needed to do this. Subsequent Presidents have since instructed other parts of the executive branch that they were not to practice racial discrimination or to deal with companies that practiced discrimination. These actions meant that the government would stop buying the products of companies that discriminated, and would not contract for services with companies or other institutions that discriminated. In 1969 President Nixon added a ban against discrimination on the basis of sex. In other words, merely by deciding how laws are to be administered, Presidents have had a great impact on American society.

In times of emergency, Presidents often claim even greater executive powers than usual. During the Civil War, Abraham Lincoln used his executive authority in a wide variety of areas. In an unusual action, he suspended the writ of habeas corpus, so that it would be easier to arrest and control those who opposed government policies. He increased the size of the Army and Navy beyond the limits set by Congress and spent millions of dollars that Congress had not appropriated. He was even able to justify the Emancipation Proclamation, which freed the slaves in rebellious states, under special war-emergency powers. Lincoln also directed the reconstruction of territories under occupation by Union forces. Similarly, during World War II, Franklin Roosevelt relied primarily on his executive authority to manage the war effort. In 1940 Roosevelt created, as part of the Executive Office of the Presidency, the Office of Emergency Management. He used the Office of Emergency Management in turn to provide the administrative framework for controlling munitions production, manpower, information, economic warfare, and many other aspects of the war effort. Of all the major agencies established to supervise the war, only one, the Office of

Price Administration, was specifically created by Congress. The rest of the wartime agencies had their legal basis in the President's executive powers.

In normal circumstances, however, the President's powers over the executive branch are considerably more restricted. Many of the restrictions come from the federal departments and agencies themselves. Most employees of the executive branch cannot be fired by the President because they work under the Civil Service Act, and that means they keep their jobs regardless of which political party has control of the White House. The people who work in these departments are often referred to as "bureaucrats," a word that implies to some, workers who are inefficient and whose ideas are hard to change. These civil servants, including those in the more important positions, often have their own ways of doing things and their own contacts with members of Congress and influential private citizens.

As an example of bureaucratic resistance to the President, we can look at an episode of John Kennedy's dealings with the State Department. Early in his term, Kennedy ordered U.S. missiles removed from Turkey because they were obsolete. The State Department, however, ignored the order and left them in Turkey because the Turkish government wanted them to stay. As a result, when the Cuban Missile Crisis occurred in 1962, Kennedy had to face complaints by the Russians that their missiles in Cuba were no closer to the U.S. than American missiles in Turkey were to the Soviet Union.

Despite such difficulties, Presidents do set the tone and direction of their Administrations. A clear example of this is presidential control of relations between government officials and the press. Presidents Johnson and Nixon both liked to control what information was given to reporters and resented having any news "leaked" to the press by subordinates. One journalist noted that it took eighteen months after Nixon took office for a White House telephone book to be prepared and released to reporters so that they would be able to reach officials easily with their questions. The journalist commented on the contrast between Nixon's approach and Jimmy Carter's. Carter had provided a complete listing of phone numbers of officials within the first months of his Administration. The journalist also found that, once in contact with officials, it was easier to get answers to questions under Carter, perhaps because Carter was more willing to let his subordinates talk to reporters.

The President also can determine the main direction in which Administration efforts will go by showing concern and interest in accomplishing certain tasks. When a President asks bureaucratic officials how they are doing against inflation, unemployment, or discrimination, for example, the officials are likely to begin to work particularly hard in these areas so that they will be able to report progress if they are asked again. Similarly, if the President demonstrates a lack of concern in certain other areas, the bureaucrats are less likely to give those areas their attention.

It is not, therefore, unreasonable to hold Presidents responsible for what the executive branch does even though they do not make every decision themselves. Lapses, of course, always happen, and no Administration is wholly free of corruption or bad judgment; in these cases it is the job of the President to punish the guilty and fire the incompetent. However, if a President fails to do this, or by neglect permits bad practices to flourish, then the Constitution expects the Congress and the electorate to hold the

President personally responsible. Indeed, if Presidents were not responsible for the executive branch, then most of the federal government would be free from its responsibility to the people.

COMMANDER IN CHIEF

The Constitution names the President commander in chief of the Armed Forces of the United States. In this capacity the President has the power to choose the top-ranking officers of the Armed Services and to determine which officers will command which military units. The President also has the responsibilities of seeing to it that U.S. military forces are adequately maintained in peacetime and are employed wisely in wartime. In fulfilling these responsibilities, it often has happened that Presidents have actually determined American foreign policy on crucial issues and have even involved the United States in foreign wars.

The problem of Presidents involving the United States in wars is not new. An early example is the U.S. war with Mexico from 1847 to 1848. Texas had won its independence from Mexico in 1836 and had been annexed to the U.S. by a joint declaration of Congress in 1845. However, Texas's borders with Mexico were a source of disagreement; Texans claimed a great deal of territory in which they had not yet settled. After the annexation of Texas by the United States, President James K. Polk sent U.S. forces into the disputed territory, and when Mexican forces opposed their entry, Polk informed Congress that a state of war existed. Congress then voted a declaration of war, but many members of Congress were unhappy about the way the matter had been handled. Former President John Quincy Adams, then sitting in the House of Representatives, complained that the Mexican War "established as an irreversible precedent that the President of the United States has but to declare that War exists, with any nation upon Earth . . . and the War is essentially declared." Abraham Lincoln, then a first-term congressman from Illinois, drew a similar conclusion. "Allow the President to invade a neighboring nation, whenever he shall deem it necessary to repel an invasion . . . and you allow him to make war at pleasure. Study to see if you can fix *any limit* to his power in this respect." Lincoln added that the Constitutional Convention had deliberately assigned the power to make war to Congress because of the tendency of executives to get involved in wars, "and they [the framers] resolved . . . that *no one man* should hold the power of bringing this oppression upon us."

In the 1960s the Vietnam War showed how accurate Lincoln's analysis was. In 1964 President Johnson told Congress and the people that U.S. ships had been attacked for no reason in the Gulf of Tonkin off Vietnam. This was not true, but it persuaded Congress and the majority of the electorate to support a general declaration in favor of retaliation against such attacks. In the fall of 1964, Johnson ran on a platform of staying out of the war in Southeast Asia and won the election against Republican Barry Goldwater on that basis. But in 1965 he sent more and more troops to Vietnam. Although Congress never voted a declaration of war and many Americans opposed U.S. involvement in the war, at one time over half a million U.S. soldiers were in Vietnam. While the war was going on, Johnson and President Nixon, who succeeded Johnson in 1969, also kept so much information secret that at the time it was hard for anyone to judge whether U.S. policy was right or not. Both Nixon and Johnson also made personal

"You mean you don't trust me?"

pledges of support to South Vietnam which were not made public at the time nor ratified by Congress; these placed the U.S. government in the position of being bound by commitments that did not have the support of the general public and had, in fact, no legal standing. The effect of these policies was to prolong the war for years at the expense of the lives of thousands of Americans and millions of Vietnamese and at the cost of billions of dollars.

The Vietnam War is the most catastrophic example of a presidential war, but it is not, as mentioned previously, the only time a President has used the power of commander in chief to push the United States toward conflict with another country. Before the U.S. entered World War I, President Woodrow Wilson ordered American merchant ships to arm themselves. After World War II broke out in Europe, Franklin Roosevelt acted even more forcefully by giving forty surplus destroyers to the British in return for military bases. And as the British became more hard-pressed, Roosevelt ordered the U.S. Navy to protect merchant ships carrying supplies to Britain until they were well across the Atlantic.

Presidential war-making powers have been used on a much smaller scale as well. In 1958 President Eisenhower sent fourteen thousand American troops to Lebanon when the political situation in that country looked unstable. In 1965 President Johnson sent twenty-two thousand troops to the Dominican Republic to intervene in a revolution there. Johnson used as his pretext the need to protect American citizens living in that country, but his real purpose was to quash what he felt was the danger of a Communist take-over. During the Vietnam War, the powers of commander in chief were used to justify extending American military activity into the territories of South Vietnam's neighbors, Laos and Cambodia.

By the 1970s the drastic increase in presidential war-making powers—particularly as exemplified by the Vietnam War—led Congress to impose some restraints upon the use of American Armed Forces. The War-Powers Act of 1973 set a limit of sixty days to any presidential commitment of American forces to combat unless Congress explicitly provided otherwise. At the time it was passed, the Act's supporters claimed it would significantly limit presidential war-making powers, but the limitation is more symbolic than real. Presidents still have the authority to commit troops to combat, which enables them to create a state of war Congress could have a hard time undoing. Despite the War-Powers Act, therefore, self-restraint by the President is the only limit against unauthorized military expeditions—and we have seen how weak a restraint that has been.

The increased independence in making war is not the only change in the nature of the President's role as commander in chief. Presidents also now take a much more active role than they used to in formulating strategy, even down to planning actual battlefield tactics. This situation is new. During the Civil War, Lincoln had trouble getting his generals to follow his strategic suggestions, and as late as World War I the main command of U.S. troops still exercised by the President was in choosing the generals to lead the American armies. Since then, however, radio and telephones have made it possible for the President to know instantly what is going on around the world and decide what measures, if any, U.S. Armed Forces should take. Atomic weapons have also increased the President's partici-

The Conference Table

pation in military decisions, because they can be used only in response to a presidential command.

This new situation has both advantages and disadvantages. It is unquestionably better for the President to be able to know more about what the Armed Forces are doing. Rapid communications make it possible to refer important decisions to Washington, where they can be made in the context of U.S. policies and interests. On the other hand, this can also tempt Presidents to spend their time making routine military decisions that probably should be left to someone else. During the Vietnam War, President Johnson often selected the bombing targets himself. This was not only a waste of his time; his personal participation in the conduct of the war probably made it harder for him to evaluate objectively U.S. involvement in the war. Instead of remaining an observer, as Presidents before him had done, Johnson was in on many of the actual combat decisions, and he came to feel a personal stake in winning. In this case, faster communications led to more unnecessary fighting rather than less.

FOREIGN POLICY

As we saw in Chapter One, the President's powers over foreign policy were carefully limited by the Constitution. The Senate was given the right to confirm the appointment of ambassadors and other diplomats, as well as the power to ratify treaties. Congress as a whole was charged with regulating foreign trade. In general, the founding fathers seem to have expected that the President would be in charge of routine matters and secret negotiations, but that Congress would share in making decisions about policy.

However, just as the President's war-making powers have

been greatly extended beyond the limits set by the Constitution, the President's control of foreign policy has also grown to far exceed the original intention of the Constitution. Today, most foreign policy decisions are made by the President or other members of the executive branch, and the involvement of Congress is very limited.

The President's power over foreign policy becomes especially apparent in crisis situations that require swift action. Perhaps the classic case of this kind is the Cuban Missile Crisis of 1962. That crisis began when American intelligence reported that the Soviet Union was installing in Cuba missiles armed with nuclear warheads. With these missiles, it would have been possible for the Russians to attack American cities with only a few minutes warning. President Kennedy felt he had to act quickly, before the missiles were armed and in place, and he had to decide even faster what steps should be taken. Some advisers advocated a bombing attack on the missile sites; others suggested that the President do nothing or that he ask for a summit meeting with Premier Nikita Khrushchev of the Soviet Union. In the end, Kennedy decided to blockade Cuba to prevent the delivery of additional missiles, and by placing pressure on Cuba and Russia, he obtained the removal of the weapons.

Independent presidential action in the Cuban Missile Crisis was justified in two ways. First, had the missiles been permitted to remain, the security of the United States would have been threatened and American prestige in the world would have been reduced. The Soviet Union might have become convinced that it could take further steps against American interests, and one of these steps could have led to war. Second, because it was felt to be essential to act before the missiles were armed, there was no time to consult Congress. Days, even hours, were important, and any time spent on public debate might increase the danger.

Fortunately, situations involving such immediate and major threats to American security only rarely arise, and presidential influence over foreign policy is usually exerted through the routine channels. Even here, though, the President's power has grown dramatically since the early days of the Republic.

There are several reasons for this change in the distribution of power over U.S. foreign policy. First, there is the increasing importance of executive decisions in making policy. An example of this power is the recognition of foreign governments. Often in American history, the recognition of a foreign government by an executive has led to important changes in foreign policy. Usually, Presidents have made the decision to recognize other governments without asking advice of Congress. In 1914 Woodrow Wilson refused to recognize the government in Mexico and used the absence of a recognized government as an excuse to send American troops there to defend American citizens. American relations with both Russia and China were interrupted by revolutions in those countries, and in each case the decision to re-establish diplomatic relations was made by the President acting alone.

The Congress has also occasionally delegated extraordinary powers to the President. In 1941 the Lend-Lease Act gave President Roosevelt the power to provide weapons to foreign countries whose security he felt was vital to U.S. interests. Roosevelt used the authority granted him to supply Britain with military supplies even before the United States entered the war, and when Germany invaded the Soviet Union, Roosevelt sent supplies to the Russians too.

The Congress has also at times given the President the right to lower U.S. tariffs below the levels set by statute, in order to allow the President to negotiate mutual tariff reductions with foreign countries. But one side effect of such actions has been to increase the President's power at the expense of Congress.

The most important increases in presidential control over foreign policy have come about by the substitution of executive agreements for official treaties to settle issues between the United States and foreign governments. An early example of this was the Rush-Bagot Convention with Britain in 1817. Richard Rush, acting Secretary of State, and Charles Bagot, a British minister in Washington, agreed between them to limit the size of American and British naval forces on the Great Lakes. President Monroe was worried that the agreement might be an intrusion upon the Senate's right to ratify treaties, so he sent the agreement to the Senate for its advice. The Senate approved it in 1818, but no treaty was ever formally drawn up. Beginning with the Administration of William McKinley, executive agreements have played a steadily increasing role in U.S. policy. McKinley used an executive agreement to establish the terms of U.S. cooperation with European powers in a military intervention in China against the Boxers. In 1905 Theodore Roosevelt approved a Japanese military protectorate over Korea by means of an executive agreement which first became known twenty years later. Franklin Roosevelt also used executive agreements in his diplomacy before the U.S. officially came into World War II. The bases-for-destroyers deal with Britain was one instance; another was the Atlantic Charter, signed by Roosevelt and Winston Churchill in August 1941. In the Charter, Roosevelt agreed to a set of goals for the postwar period. Near

Back where it belongs

the end of the war, Roosevelt reached executive agreement with Churchill and Joseph Stalin at the Yalta Convention on a variety of issues concerning the conduct of the war and the postwar order.

However, the greatest use of executive agreements has come since World War II. As the United States began to install permanent military bases around the world, executive agreements were used to obtain leases of these bases in return for a promise of American aid. Many other issues concerning American relations with overseas allies were also regulated by executive agreements. This procedure, which seemed necessary to U.S. security in the 1950s and early 1960s, began to be questioned by the late 1960s, largely because of the Vietnam War. Members of Congress objected that while the President conducted war and moved U.S. soldiers around the world at will, he presented to the Senate only treaties dealing with relatively minor issues such as copyright, stamp collecting, and shrimp fishing. Often it was difficult for Congress even to find out what the President had promised a foreign country. To remedy this situation, a law was enacted in 1972 requiring the President to inform Congress within sixty days of concluding any executive agreement.

Obviously, Presidents will find ways to make secret promises when they feel secrecy is essential. For example verbal agreements could be made instead of written ones. The real question is the extent to which Presidents should be entirely independent of Congress in conducting foreign policy.

The Vietnam War showed that the Constitution was farsighted in providing that foreign affairs be divided between the President and Congress. There are, to be sure, occasionally situations in which it is necessary for the President to act with great secrecy or great speed. But these crises are rare, and, as the Constitution suggests, presidential policies need to be scrutinized carefully by Congress and ordinary citizens. Presidential mistakes ought to be detected before they result in unwise promises to foreign countries or even war. Then, even if a war does come, citizens will at least know why they are fighting.

POLITICAL LEADER

When the Constitution was written, there were no political parties such as we have today. These developed soon after, however, and by 1800 the President was also the leader of a political party. In the nineteenth century the practice developed of having parties name candidates for the Presidency instead of encouraging individuals to run independently, on their own merit and without regard for political affiliation. This practice has helped change the way Americans think about their Presidents. The skilled executive imagined by the Constitutional Convention is much less important today than the politician who promises to favor certain policies and oppose others. Presidents are expected to have a platform or programs they support, and we vote for Presidents on the basis of what they propose to do.

The politicization of the Presidency has affected the way we see our Presidents as well as our presidential candidates. Often it is hard to tell whether a President is acting out of a personal interest or out of conviction that a certain policy is right for the country. For example, Presidents are always tempted to adopt policies that will lead to prosperity in the year they intend to seek re-election, even if those policies may have detrimental long-term effects on the economy. Thus, the boom encouraged by President Nixon in 1972 resulted in higher rates of inflation after he left office. Sometimes, even foreign policy decisions may be influenced by politics. In 1972 President Nixon made highly dramatic visits to Russia and China; both of the trips were given extensive coverage by television and the press. Moreover, shortly before the election, Nixon's Secretary of State, Henry Kissinger, announced a breakthrough in the Vietnam peace negotiations.

Despite the importance of politics in the Presidency, Presidents are rarely able to command the unanimous support of politicians in their own party. For example, in 1937 Franklin Roosevelt was opposed by many Democrats in Congress when he tried to change the composition of the Supreme Court. Similarly, the most vocal opponents of Johnson's war policies during the Johnson Administration were other Democrats. Moreover, when the President takes actions that appear to attack the interests of a particular region or locality, the congressional representatives of those districts frequently criticize the President's decisions regardless of whether or not they belong to the same party as the President. In 1977, when President Carter took steps to cancel certain dam-building projects, he met opposition from many Democratic senators and representatives from the regions affected by the cutbacks. Because of this, it often happens that presidential proposals are sharply criticized or even ignored in spite of the fact that the President's party may have a large majority in Congress.

Such situations can develop because the President has relatively few formal ties to the party apart from having been nominated by it. The President does name the party's national chairperson, who supervises the party organization and tries to see that everything is run to the

The Globe Trotter

President's satisfaction. However, the President has little influence over who is chosen to run for other offices, and it often happens that opponents of presidential policies are elected to important offices. Occasionally, Presidents have tried to change this by urging voters to defeat or elect certain candidates. The most famous instance of this occurred in 1938 when Franklin Roosevelt tried to "purge" the Democratic party in the primaries. The effort was unsuccessful, and most of the men Roosevelt asked the voters to defeat retained their seats.

The looseness of party ties in America is very different from the situation in most other democratic countries. Wherever the head of government is a Prime Minister elected by the legislative branch, party ties and party discipline are very tight. In such situations, the Prime Minister can almost always count on the support of other members of his or her party to pass whatever legislation the government proposes. In the United States, however, party affiliation rarely connects the executive and legislative branches. One historian has argued that we ought to think of American politics as consisting of four parties: congressional and presidential Republicans, and congressional and presidential Democrats.

Because Presidents cannot automatically rely upon the support of members of their own party in Congress, they often have to turn to the opposition party to fill important or sensitive posts in the government in order to involve them in policies that might easily be criticized. President Johnson, for example, named Republican Henry Cabot Lodge to serve as ambassador to Vietnam, and President Nixon chose Democrat John Connally to be Secretary of the Treasury. The coalition between the President and the opposition party can sometimes go further than this. President Eisenhower relied heavily on Democratic support in Congress to enact his programs, especially after 1954, when the Democrats took control of both houses of Congress.

The President's political position is, therefore, extremely complex. Although nominated by a political party and elected with the assistance of that party's local organizations, the President neither controls the party nor is always opposed by members of the other party. To a great extent, this arrangement means that the President operates at a level removed from politics, and that ability to lead depends more on personal qualities than on party affiliations.

CHAPTER FOUR

The Exercise of Presidential Power

Thus far, we have said a great deal about the different tasks a President performs, but not much about how the President performs them. A good way to get an idea of the President's daily responsibilities is to take a look at the six days novelist John Hersey spent with President Ford in 1975 to get material for his book *The President*.

THE PRESIDENT'S DAYS

According to Hersey, President Ford worked about twelve hours a day in the White House office. He spent an hour or two of that time in meetings with his aides on foreign policy; in other weeks the meetings might have been with the Secretary of State. Hersey did not attend these meetings but believed that during them the President was probably briefed on current developments and presented with decisions to make or approve. There were also staff meetings every day with specialists and advisers on domestic issues, such as defense, energy, and the economy. These meetings had the purpose of keeping the President informed so that he could decide what policies he wanted to follow, and they also gave him the chance to check up on programs that were already in progress.

In addition to these policy-making or administrative meetings, Ford devoted a large amount of time to public relations. He met every day with the White House press secretary to pass along information he wanted released to the public and to discuss answers to questions reporters were likely to ask. Ford himself made several public appearances and spoke to several different groups: a short talk to a group of small-town newspaper editors, a humorous address to a banquet held by a journalists' group, and an interview with the editors of *Fortune* magazine. These appearances kept Ford in the news and helped him present a favorable public image. In the course of the week the President also met several times with his advisers to plan speeches he was scheduled to give in future weeks, so that his speechwriters could start to work on them.

Some of Ford's time, of course, was devoted to purely ceremonial events. In the week Hersey was with him, Ford was visited by Miss America, the Maid of Cotton, the winners of a high school contest sponsored by the Veterans of Foreign Wars, the Easter Seal poster girl, a delegation of the Gridiron Club (to which most of the Washington news corps belonged), a delegation of food officials from the Soviet Union, and a barbershop quartet. Few of these meetings took more than thirty minutes, but more time might have been spent if, as in other weeks, there was a foreign dignitary to be welcomed or entertained.

Finally, Ford spent a great deal of time trying to get support for his policies. This is one of the most difficult things for any President to do. Many people must be persuaded that the President's policies are the right ones. Much of the effort put into public relations, in fact, has as its real objective winning support for the President's policies, and in the week we are discussing, Ford also met privately with business and labor leaders, members of Congress, and members of the federal bureaucracy—all in search of support for his policies. Of all the things Hersey observed that week, two stood out as having seemed particularly important. First was the way President Ford gathered information and decided what policies he wanted to pursue. Second was the way Ford tried to persuade other people to do what he felt should be done.

POLICY-MAKING

"Policy" is a term used to describe a general objective of government. Policies can be fairly broad, such as the defense of Israel's sovereignty, the promotion of economic growth, or the protection of the environment from pollution. However, since almost everyone would agree that the safety of Israel, a cleaner environment, and economic prosperity are desirable things, the methods proposed to reach these goals are really the policies the President must fight for. For example, a policy of protecting the environment by offering tax deductions to those who cooperate is different from trying to protect the environment through regulations requiring compliance to government standards. To be meaningful, therefore, presidential policies have to be fairly specific.

Policy-making is an area where a President's character

and beliefs really come into play. This is true because the President often has to decide between two objectives that are both important but that cannot both be accomplished at the same time. Does the President want to control inflation, the rising cost of living, even if it means some people will lose their jobs? Or does the President want to reduce the number of people out of work even if it means inflation will result? Does the President think government should be active in protecting people from discrimination or that it should intervene only when ordered to act by the courts? In foreign affairs, a President might have to decide between taking a strong public position or working quietly toward a peaceful compromise. Dilemmas such as these are faced constantly by Presidents when they are called on to judge actions by parts of the executive branch, to decide how to spend tax money, or to determine what legislation to propose to Congress. Often the President's own values determine which alternative is chosen.

The first step in policy-making is the gathering of information. It might seem that Presidents would have no trouble getting information. After all, as we have already seen, many people work directly for the President at the White House, and the departments and agencies of the executive branch are obliged to answer any questions the President might have. Many people outside of government are also eager to assist with any presidential inquiry and are flattered by an invitation to help. Moreover, Presidents often like to encourage the impression that they have all the available information, "all the facts," meaning to suggest that their opponents do not and would agree with the President's policies if they did.

However, the very abundance of information available poses something of a problem for the President; there is simply too much for any one person to make use of. The usual solution to this problem is to hire White House assistants who spend their time summarizing information for the President. This is not always bad; no President really needs to know how much money is spent on electricity at Fort Polk or how many people the Department of Agriculture employs in Iowa. What the President does need to know are not facts of this kind; he or she needs evaluations, opinions, and educated guesses. What are the political factions in China and how will U.S. trade proposals affect Chinese politics? What will an unbalanced budget do to inflation or unemployment? No one knows these things for certain in the way the Fort Polk electricity bill can be known, but Presidents often need to estimate economic consequences or how people will respond to certain actions before they decide their policies. The problem for Presidents, therefore, is not really to get all the facts, but to get the best advice.

Sometimes the nature of the Presidency works against the President getting good advice. George Reedy, an assistant to President Johnson, pointed out that nearly everyone with whom the President deals wants the President's good opinion. Presidential aides, for example, are usually eager to please their boss and try to collect facts and opinions that support what they think the President wants to hear. People from outside the White House are often impressed with the power of the Presidency, and their respect for the office often encourages them to offer only mild criticisms of presidential policies. Presidents, moreover, like other people, often simply don't listen to people who disagree with them. As a result, sometimes Presidents will not find out things they don't want to hear, even though these are often the things they most need to know.

President Johnson, Reedy says, frequently tested his ideas with many staff people, found they all agreed with him, and only later discovered that there were a great number of people outside the White House who opposed his suggestions. One example of this was Johnson's plan to unite the Department of Labor and the Department of Commerce. After many consultations with members of the executive branch, Johnson decided that the idea was a good one. Only after announcing his intention did he learn that both labor and business leaders were strongly opposed to it. As a result of their opposition, the project never got off the ground in Congress. A more serious instance was the Vietnam War, which was supported by Presidents Johnson and Nixon long after many citizens and members of Congress had come to feel it was wrong.

We will suppose, however, that the President has gotten a variety of opinions and decided knowledgeably upon a policy. What happens then? How does he or she persuade other people that the policy is right?

PRESIDENTIAL PERSUASION

To carry out most of their policies, Presidents need the support and cooperation of many people. There are, to be sure, a few exceptions to this rule. Presidents can, for example, replace government officials who have opposed them or use federal troops to control rioting. They can also veto bills passed by Congress, knowing that in most cases Congress will not be able to override the veto. These exercises of presidential power are essentially negative, however, and can be applied only in special circumstances.

In general, the President's ability to influence people

depends on two things: prestige with the public and professional reputation as an able politician and administrator.

By "public prestige" is meant the President's standing with the voting public. This standing changes all the time. Public opinion polls reveal something about it, but not everything. The term "professional reputation" describes the President's standing with other politicians and officials, which depends mostly on how loyal the President is to the policies he or she decides on and the energy with which these policies are carried out. This is important because politicians do not like to spend their time and effort on programs they think the President may abandon. If a President is consistent, therefore, other politicians will be more willing to support presidential policies.

We can understand how important public prestige and professional reputation are if we remember who the President must deal with every day. First, there are the federal bureaucrats, who may or may not have to be persuaded to accept the President's priorities. Sometimes private businesses, groups, or individuals will have to be persuaded to help with one of the President's projects. Finally, if legislation is required or appropriations are needed for a project, the President will have to persuade Congress to go along.

It may be surprising to see federal bureaucrats included among the people whose help the President needs. After all, as head of the executive branch the President is their superior and is entitled to set the policy under which they work. In practice, however, the President must often first win the support of other members of the executive branch in order to persuade the public and Congress to support presidential policies.

Executive officials can seriously embarrass the President when they disapprove of a policy. An example of this can be seen from the Nixon Administration. In October 1973, Nixon decided to fire Special Prosecutor Archibald Cox, who had subpoenaed some White House tapes for his investigation of the Watergate Affair. Cox was a subordinate of Attorney General Elliot Richardson. Richardson refused to fire Cox, however, because he had personally guaranteed Congress that Cox would be able to conduct his investigation without interference, and he resigned when Nixon ordered him to remove Cox. Richardson's assistant, William Ruckelshaus, allowed himself to be fired rather than fire Cox. The third-ranking official in the Justice Department finally did fire Cox, but by this time it was clear to the public and Congress that Nixon was trying to get rid of Cox for personal reasons. Public pressure and impeachment resolutions introduced in the House of Representatives forced Nixon to agree to the appointment of another special prosecutor to continue Cox's work.

This episode, which became known as the Saturday Night Massacre because it occurred on a Saturday night, shows how officials can embarrass a President by resigning or otherwise opposing presidential orders in public. It also shows how important public prestige can be in the President's dealings with other members of the executive branch. When the event occurred, Nixon's popularity had already reached a new low due to months of disclosures about how White House assistants had obstructed justice. Since so many people already doubted Nixon's personal honesty, Richardson and Ruckelshaus could be sure their actions would have a great impact. If Nixon had been more popular, they might have been less willing to make their disagreements known. Thus, Nixon's poor public standing made him more vulnerable to criticism from within his own Administration.

Such dramatics do not happen often, but there are ways in which federal officials can oppose a President's policies more quietly. They can, for example, give information to Congress or to the press that contradicts what the President has said or proposed. Military officials often give their friends in Congress their own estimates of Soviet military strength if the President tries to reduce the budget for weapons. During the Vietnam War, employees of the government who opposed U.S. policies sometimes leaked news of secret bombings to the press. Presidential aides have always been very critical of unauthorized disclosures such as these because they undermine executive control of information to Congress and the public.

Another incident shows the importance of professional reputation to a President. In 1975 President Ford announced his support for a labor bill that was before Congress and encouraged John Dunlop, his Secretary of Labor, to work for its passage. The bill passed Congress, but after it was enacted, Ford changed his mind and vetoed it. Dunlop resigned out of embarrassment. More important for Ford, however, was that his reversal made other politicians wary that they too might be left out on a limb when it became necessary to lean on him for support.

The President must also occasionally be able to persuade or win support from private individuals in order to implement his or her policies. One example of this is presidential intervention in labor disputes. The purpose of these interventions is usually to prevent strikes in vital industries or to arrange labor contracts that are anti-inflationary. In 1962 President Kennedy gave a dramatic demonstration of this kind of activity. He had persuaded steel workers to accept a contract with low wage increases in order to prevent inflation, but after the contract was signed, the largest steel companies raised their prices anyway. Kennedy denounced the steel companies in a press conference and announced plans to purchase steel for government use only from companies that did not raise their prices. The major steel companies believed this threat because of Kennedy's reputation for carrying through his announced intentions and thus they reduced prices to the earlier level.

One of the most important tests of the President's powers of persuasion is in relation to Congress. In addition to trying to persuade Congress to enact or change federal laws, every President must submit an annual budget to Congress. Congress can raise or lower this budget and even change how the money in it is to be spent. In this way, Congress has the opportunity to review nearly every part of the President's program. Congress also has the power to conduct investigations into the operation of the executive branch or into the President's personal activities.

It is not surprising, then, that Presidents try to influence what Congress does. It is not unusual for at least several White House aides to spend all their time meeting with members of Congress in order to explain what the President wants done and asking for their support. Presidents usually have close personal relations with many members of Congress, and members of Congress are often called by the President on the telephone or invited to the White House to discuss matters. However, Presidents can generally rely on the congressional leaders of their political parties to support their policies.

In dealing with Congress, it is definitely helpful for the President to have wide popular support. This can persuade many members of Congress that their constituents support the President's program. Popular support can be especially valuable if the President is up for re-election. Members of Congress are naturally more reluctant to antagonize a President who will be around for a long time than one who is about to leave office.

In addition to establishing personal contacts and acquiring popular support, the President must gain a reputation for sticking to promises in order to get support in Congress. Members of Congress do not like to look foolish in front of their constituents by doing favors for the President and then having the President lose interest in their project.

FOREIGN POLICY

Foreign policy differs from domestic policy in that it is usually conducted more secretly, and since war can result from errors in judgment, the stakes are higher. However, the steps in making foreign policy are basically the same as those we have just discussed. Just as with domestic issues, there are many different choices in foreign policy. How much government money should be spent or how many lives risked to protect property of private U.S. companies in foreign countries? Should the U.S. help keep "friendly" dictators in power by sending them weapons and foreign aid? Should the U.S. try to overthrow other governments? There are no clearcut answers to questions like these. The way a President decides on policy depends a great deal on his or her character and beliefs.

The *Mayaguez* incident is a good example of how a President's character can affect foreign policy. The *Mayaguez* was a U.S. freighter that had sailed too close to Cambodia in 1975. It was seized by the new Communist government of Cambodia and held captive. Thirty-nine Americans made up the crew. The new Cambodian government was disorganized, and communications with it were somewhat difficult. After a few days of negotiations, President Ford and Henry Kissinger, his Secretary of State, decided not to wait any longer. They believed that American prestige, at a low point as a result of the takeover of both Cambodia and Vietnam by the Communists, required a show of U.S. military strength. So they sent marines to the island where the crew was being kept. The prisoners were freed, but more than fifty U.S. military men died or were wounded in the operation.

Another example of how a President's character can affect foreign policy was Jimmy Carter's campaign in the area of human rights. Carter, perhaps due to his strong religious upbringing, wanted as President to pursue a "moral" foreign policy. He therefore decided that the U.S. government would speak out against human rights violations in Russia, racial separation policies in South Africa, and governments such as those of Chile and Brazil that imprisoned political opponents and inflicted other harsh punishments on them. This was a significant break from the policies of Presidents Nixon and Ford and Secretary of State Kissinger. These men had favored less public criticism of other countries' internal affairs.

In order to make decisions about foreign policy, Presidents must keep up to date with what is going on in the world. The State Department and intelligence services constantly collect information, and a summary of this information is given to the President every day. The President also receives foreign and domestic newspapers. In a crisis such as the *Mayaguez* incident, the President will be given reports several times a day. Analyses of situations by subordinates are not always accurate, of course, so the

"Just ignore it;
there are no holes in this thing!"

President has to evaluate them in the same way as advice about domestic policies.

When a policy has been chosen, the President must usually get the support of Congress in order to make the policy effective. The role of Congress is most obvious when a treaty has been negotiated and must be ratified by the Senate. The President must be able to persuade a two-thirds majority of the Senate to vote for the treaty. A famous instance of failure to do this was the Senate's refusal to ratify the Treaty of Versailles, negotiated at the end of World War I. Woodrow Wilson had gone personally to Paris to participate in the negotiations for the treaty, and at his insistence the treaty had incorporated his plans for a League of Nations. The League, Wilson felt, could act as a body against any nation that started a war in the future and in this way could help preserve world peace. The Senate, however, refused to ratify the treaty, and the United States never joined the League of Nations. Wilson's policy failed at least in part because of his inability to gain support in the Senate. Subsequent Presidents, having learned from Wilson's experience, have included members of Congress on teams sent to negotiate treaties.

A recent instance of presidential success in this area was the 1978 treaty between the United States and Panama. Panama wanted greater control of the Panama Canal. President Carter wanted a treaty which gave them greater control ratified as a sign that the United States was willing to pay attention to the concerns of smaller, less powerful nations. Many people in the United States were against the treaty, however, and a large number of senators opposed ratification. Carter and his legislative aides had to work very hard to win support in the Senate. If the Senate had rejected the treaty, Carter would have found it harder to negotiate future agreements with other countries. The treaty was eventually ratified, with one vote to spare.

Treaties are not the only instance where the President must seek congressional support in foreign policy. Special legislation sometimes must be enacted for trade negotiations to take place between the United States and foreign countries. Since tariffs and other controls on foreign trade are established by legislation, not executive action, the President must be authorized by Congress before he or she can reach trading agreements with other nations or trading groups such as the European Common Market. President Kennedy wanted to reduce trade barriers in the early 1960s, but he had to work very hard to get the authority to do it, because at that time reduction of barriers to trade was opposed by many business and labor groups that feared competition from foreign industries.

Presidents may also find it necessary to work to maintain their authority over the bureaucracies within the government in order to prevent dissatisfied bureaucrats from undercutting presidential foreign policies. A particularly striking instance of a bureaucracy making major decisions on its own was the Central Intelligence Agency's efforts in the 1960s to have Fidel Castro of Cuba assassinated. These assassination attempts seem to have been undertaken without President Kennedy's knowledge or approval, but they did reflect what the CIA thought the U.S. policy should be. More often, obstruction of presidential policies by bureaucrats is accomplished by leaking classified materials and documents to the press. The most celebrated case of this kind involved a history of the U.S. involvement in Vietnam prepared by the Pentagon in the late 1960s. When President Nixon appeared to have decided to continue the war, former federal employee Daniel Ellsberg provided copies of the history, called *The Pentagon Papers,* to the *New York Times* and the *Washington Post,* which published long excerpts despite efforts by the Nixon Administration to have publication blocked. The excerpts revealed that the American public and Congress had been deceived by the U.S. government. Nixon's inability to retain the confidence of his officials, therefore, helped undermine his capacity for implementing his policies.

CHAPTER FIVE

The Restraint of Presidential Power

As we have seen, the Constitutional Convention carefully divided responsibilities for the federal government between the President and Congress. Most of the members of the Convention probably thought, as Madison did, that the main threat to this balance was likely to come from Congress. In the twentieth century, however, it has been the Presidency that has emerged as the essential threat to constitutional balance.

There are many reasons for this shift. The executive branch of government has grown faster than the ability of Congress to supervise it. Television news, in particular, which feeds on visually dramatic events, has focused public attention on the President—who *does* something every day, even if it is only to receive the Easter Seal girl in the White House. Congress, whose work consists mainly of discussion and resolution, is often ignored. Furthermore, in the 1950s and 1960s most people thought foreign affairs should be conducted with great secrecy and great speed, and this also worked in favor of the President.

Two major results of this trend were the Vietnam War and the Watergate Affair. The war was waged at least partly in secret by the executive branch, and many attempts by Congress to wind down the war were altogether ignored by the President. American involvement in Indochina dated back to the 1940s, but it was only in 1965 that American troops were sent to Vietnam in large numbers. President Johnson depended solely on his executive power to take this action; he did not seek a declaration of war from Congress, and he went back on his own campaign promise in 1964 to keep the United States out of war in Asia. *The Pentagon Papers*, mentioned earlier, revealed that justifications for the war presented at the time by Johnson and his aides were often designed to deliberately deceive Congress and the public about the nature of the war. The war was continued by Richard Nixon, who succeeded Johnson as President after promising in the election campaign of 1968 to end the war; U.S. participation in the conflict didn't end until 1973.

The other major misuse of presidential power, the Watergate Affair, began with the discovery of a break-in and attempted bugging of Democratic party offices by employees of the Nixon re-election organization in 1972. The scandal eventually came to envelop Nixon personally because of his actions and those of his aides to conceal their involvement in the break-in, and because many of those associated with the break-in later confessed to having committed other illegal actions on behalf of the Nixon White House. Nixon resigned to avoid impeachment after it had become apparent that he as President had used the

powers of his office to harass political opponents and monitor their activities and to illegally obtain and misuse political campaign contributions.

The Vietnam War and Watergate had the ultimate effect of making it clear that restraints upon the Presidency were and are necessary. Watergate in particular showed that impeachment was still a viable weapon to call to task an unscrupulous President. Before considering the restraint of impeachment more closely, however, it is important to review some of the routine restraints on the President, such as Congress's budgetary and investigatory powers, the Senate's right to reject presidential appointees and to ratify treaties, and one that has not been mentioned earlier, the Supreme Court.

THE PRESIDENT AND CONGRESS

Congress can force changes in presidential policies in a number of ways. If the President introduces new legislation, Congress can pass that legislation in a different form or refuse to pass it at all. Even a President with substantial majorities in both houses of Congress can run into these difficulties. Among Jimmy Carter's highest priorities in the first years of his Administration were an energy conservation program and a major reform of federal tax policies. But the heavily Democratic Congress showed little interest in these proposals and did not pass major legislation concerning them. Further, in 1978, Congress forced Carter to accept a lower tax reduction than he had initially requested.

Congress can also enact legislation over a presidential veto, thus establishing as law policies that the President does not agree with. President Truman vetoed the Taft-Hartley bill regulating strikes because he felt the bill placed too much pressure on labor unions but not enough on businesses to resolve disputes that could lead to strikes. Congress, however, passed the bill over his objections. In 1973, Congress passed over a Nixon veto a war-powers bill that set limits on presidential authority to order U.S. troops into combat. Nixon believed the bill would dangerously restrict the power of the President to be effective in world affairs. But Congress, remembering the Vietnam War, decided otherwise.

Less dramatic but more important than any of these methods of altering presidential policies is congressional authority over the national budget. Budget-making is one of the ways Congress truly influences national policies. Much of policy-making is showing preference for one desirable project over another, and every year the President presents to Congress a budget that incorporates his or her particular priorities. However, the President's budget is not legally binding, and the national budget is not written into law until Congress approves the expenditures and appropriates the money to pay for them.

Congress can alter the President's budget in many ways. It can increase Social Security payments, raise the salaries of federal employees, or increase or decrease allocations of funds to the different government agencies. It can reduce or raise the sums that the President proposes to spend for defense, for school aid, or for food stamps, for example. Sometimes Congress deliberately acts to prohibit certain proposed expenditures, as it did when it refused to finance the building of a supersonic transport plane that President Nixon had pushed for in the early 1970s. Funding decisions such as these can advance or kill any federal project and are one of the main ways Congress limits the President's ability to shape national policy to his or her own objectives.

The power Congress has over the budget can also be used to restrain the President from undesirable overseas involvements. For example, in 1976 President Ford secretly sent military equipment to aid anti-Communist forces in a civil war in Angola. When news of the action was leaked, Congress investigated and decided that the aid should be cut off before it led to an American involvement there similar to the one in Vietnam. Congress enforced its decision by stipulating that no money in the budget could be allocated as aid to the Angolans.

Congressional budgetary authority is such an important restraint on the Presidency that President Nixon tried to circumvent it during his Administration. Nixon could not spend money that Congress had not appropriated, but he could and did refuse to spend money that Congress had appropriated for programs he did not like. This procedure, which is known as impoundment of funds, was eventually ruled unconstitutional by the Supreme Court.

Congress can also restrain presidential exercise of power by use of its investigatory powers. The Constitution gives to Congress the right to gather information it needs to enact laws, and this right is often interpreted to mean that Congress can investigate the activities of the federal government itself. For example, during the Vietnam War the Senate Foreign Relations Committee held hearings on the government's policies and the objectives of the war, and forced representatives of the Administration to present and defend its conduct of the war. Congress also frequently investigates the competency and honesty of the various federal agencies, and Presidents must take care to see that agencies under their jurisdiction are well run or face political embarrassment from these congressional inquiries.

The Senate also exercises special controls over the President by its right to ratify treaties and confirm presidential appointments. As we have already seen, the right to ratify treaties is less important than it used to be, because much foreign policy is conducted through executive agreements, which do not require ratification. Indeed, many of these executive agreements are kept secret, at least in their details, and are beyond scrutiny by the Senate or anyone else.

The right to confirm appointees, however, remains an important control upon presidential power. Often the knowledge that their appointments will be subject to scrutiny by the Senate forces Presidents to be careful about whom they name to federal office. But rejections of presidential appointments still do occur. In modern times the Senate used this power most dramatically when it turned down two of Richard Nixon's appointments to the Supreme Court because the men named had racist backgrounds and lacked distinguished records as judges. Ultimately, Nixon named other judges whose records were less questionable.

CONGRESSIONAL RESTRAINTS AND EXECUTIVE PRIVILEGE

To be effective, congressional restraints require that there be a free flow of information from the President to Congress. Congress can act intelligently on budget requests, for example, only if it can get a clear picture of how each agency is doing its job. Similarly, Congress cannot investigate the executive branch without the cooperation of the officials involved; if the President instructs these officials to refuse to answer questions, then the congressional inquiry will have great difficulty proceeding. Finally, the Senate cannot advise the President on foreign policy if agreements are made by the President alone and are kept secret.

In recent years, Presidents have often refused to provide Congress with information on the grounds of "executive privilege," and this refusal has undermined the ability of the Congress to contain presidential power. It should be noted that claims of executive privilege were not always, nor even usually, based on a need to protect national security. Presidents have often claimed to be protecting the privacy of individuals who would be embarrassed if certain information became public, or have also often argued that they were honoring the constitutional division of powers. The most common argument, however, has been that secrecy is necessary because without it, it would be impossible to have free debates over policy within the executive branch.

None of the first Presidents withheld information from Congress on the basis of executive privilege. It was first claimed in 1833 by Andrew Jackson, who contended that his personal conversations with his assistants were confidential. Jackson admitted, however, that Congress had the right to any information it might consider necessary if it were investigating charges of presidential misconduct. Subsequent Presidents also occasionally withheld information, but it was not until 1954 that a President—President Eisenhower—asserted the right of any President to deny Congress access to information from any part of the executive branch. The doctrine of executive privilege is, therefore, of fairly recent origin.

Since Eisenhower claimed executive privilege as a general rule, many congressional inquiries have been refused. The effect of this policy has been to interfere with the ability of Congress to oversee the executive branch. Often, the requests for information were turned down by officials of less than Cabinet rank. In some cases assertions of executive privilege have been used to cover up mistakes or scandals by preventing the facts from becoming known. In an extreme case, President Nixon even tried to claim executive privilege to prevent Congress from investigating his personal misconduct in an impeachment inquiry, although the Constitution explicitly gives Congress the right to conduct such investigations. These instances involved no foreign danger to the U.S. government, and the only people whose security was being protected were officials of the executive branch.

One of the most important areas affected by the doctrine of executive privilege has been the area of foreign affairs. So much of the day-to-day conduct of foreign policy is in the hands of the executive branch that congressional review is particularly important in this field. Presidents have often made that review very difficult to accomplish, however, by refusing documents or information or by simply delaying delivery of information for a long time without ever formally refusing to hand it over. Moreover, since so much U.S. foreign policy is conducted by personal aides of the President, Presidents can keep Congress in the dark about foreign affairs by refusing to let their aides testify before congressional committees. When executive privilege is used in this way, it can even become difficult for Congress to find out exactly what the President's policies are.

The classification of official secrets, operating under the authority of the President, can also interfere with serious debate on foreign policy. For example, in 1969 and 1970 the Nixon Administration conducted a secret bombing war in Cambodia. It was, of course, known to the Cambodians, who were being attacked, but it was not known to the people in the United States. Not only was the conduct of the

"He has a very important job in
the State Department. He denies things."

war kept from the electorate but also from congressional committees, who were repeatedly lied to and presented with false information. Similar problems developed in 1975, when there were congressional investigations of the CIA. The congressional committees were having a very difficult time finding out just what the CIA was doing; often, when they would request documents, the executive branch would refuse to provide them. This made it hard for the committees to frame legislation to prevent the CIA from abusing its power. A truly thorough congressional investigation became possible only after journalists uncovered previously secret CIA operations.

There are, to be sure, situations in which secrets should be kept, at least for a few years. The question, however, is whether the President and the executive branch should have the sole power to decide which secrets ought to be kept and which ought to be shared. As with executive privilege, excessive classification of information as secret can have the effect of hiding the errors of the executive branch and making public debate difficult or even impossible. A reasonable compromise would be for the President to share information unreservedly with congressional committees. This was the policy adopted by President Roosevelt in World War II, who kept Congress informed of even secret operations, including the development of the atomic bomb. A compromise such as this has the advantage of allowing Congress to restrain the natural tendency of the executive branch to conceal its own mistakes and inefficiency.

As desirable as a limitation of executive privilege is, it is possible to achieve only if Congress is supported by the public when it attempts to unlock the secrets of the executive branch. The public must be suspicious of Presidents who claim that congressional inquiries are posing risks to national security or who set out to embarrass members of Congress trying to find out what the federal government is doing. Without public support, members of Congress will be forced to accept all assertions of the President.

THE PRESIDENT AND
THE SUPREME COURT

The Supreme Court has less occasion to deal with political issues than Congress and therefore comes into conflict with the President far less frequently than either the House of Representatives or the Senate. There have been some instances, however, where the Supreme Court has acted to set clear restraints on presidential authority. The Court's power to declare laws unconstitutional can negate important portions of a President's program. The Court can also restore to individuals rights that have been taken away by presidential action, or can interpret the law in such a way as to force Presidents to act contrary to their own inclinations.

The most famous example of the Supreme Court's interference with presidential programs occurred during the 1930s, when Franklin Roosevelt was President. Roosevelt proposed, and Congress enacted, a number of laws to relieve the crisis caused by the Great Depression. The Supreme Court declared a number of these "New Deal" statutes unconstitutional, including part of the National Industrial Recovery Act, which was the basis of Roosevelt's economic program. In that decision, handed down in 1935, the Court ruled that Roosevelt had overstepped congressional power to regulate interstate commerce. Roosevelt called the Supreme Court ruling a "horse and buggy" interpretation of the interstate commerce clause of the Constitution. After he won re-election in 1936 with a landslide victory over Republican Alf Landon, Roosevelt sent a bill to Congress that would have permitted him to name additional Justices to the Supreme Court who would be favorable to New Deal programs. But this "Court-packing" proposal failed in Congress, and the attempt to challenge the Court's power cost Roosevelt popular support in many parts of the country. The Supreme Court did, however, modify its own position in response to the pressure of public opinion by approving other New Deal legislation, and eventually Roosevelt was able to bring in a number of his own Justices to replace those who were retiring.

The Supreme Court's actions in relation to the New Deal were special because those actions attacked the heart of Roosevelt's program. But many Presidents have suffered minor setbacks when an isolated action or a particular piece of legislation was declared unconstitutional. In 1952, during the Korean War, President Harry Truman ordered seizure of the nation's steel mills to avert a strike after negotiations between the steel union and the steel companies had broken down. Truman reasoned that the nation could not afford a fall-off of steel production in the middle of a war, and that government seizure, which deprived the union of pay raises and the steel companies of profits, would be the best way to force both sides to reach an agreement. But the companies appealed to the Supreme Court, claiming that the President and his agent, Secretary of Commerce Charles Sawyer, had exceeded the authority given them by Congress and the Constitution. The Supreme Court ruled on behalf of the steel companies, and Truman had to return the mills to them. The union then struck, and the settlement finally reached after a long strike provided for substantially higher price increases than Truman had wanted.

The Supreme Court also played an important role in the Watergate Affair, which forced Richard Nixon to resign the Presidency. When Archibald Cox was named special prosecutor in the summer of 1973 to investigate charges that members of the Nixon Administration had participated in a cover-up involving the wiretapping of Democratic party offices, he subpoenaed tape recordings made in Nixon's office of conversations between Nixon and his assistants. Nixon resisted the subpoena, claiming the tapes were protected by executive privilege, but in October 1973 the Supreme Court upheld the special prosecutor's request and ordered Nixon to hand over the tapes. This order provoked the Saturday Night Massacre, mentioned earlier. Following the popular and congressional outcry over Cox's dismissal, Nixon eventually did hand over the tapes, and the evidence in them became an important part of the House Judiciary Committee's case to impeach Nixon. Then, in the summer of 1974, the Supreme Court ordered Nixon to supply additional tapes to Leon Jaworski, Cox's successor as special prosecutor; this material contained conclusive evidence of Nixon's participation in the cover-up.

Both the New Deal and the steel cases involved Supreme Court decisions nullifying presidential actions, but occasionally the Supreme Court can force Presidents to act in situations where they would prefer to remain on the sidelines. The 1954 Court decision ordering desegregation of the nation's public schools is an example. President Eisenhower was not personally enthusiastic about school desegregation, and he hoped to stay out of the disputes that followed the ruling of the Court. In 1957, however, the school district of Little Rock, Arkansas, was ordered to desegregate one of its high schools, and, as we have seen, the governor of Arkansas, Orval Faubus, defiantly sent National Guardsmen to prevent black students from entering. When the National Guard was withdrawn by order of a local federal judge, a crowd of citizens gathered to prevent the integration of the school. Faubus took no action to disperse the crowd. Eisenhower had tried earlier to persuade Faubus at an informal meeting in Newport, Rhode Island, to drop his opposition to integration, but he had not been successful. The overt defiance of the federal Court order compelled Eisenhower to take action. He had the Secretary of the Army send regular U.S. Army troops to Little Rock to enforce the integration order. One of Eisenhower's aides later wrote that this dispatch of troops to Little Rock was "the most repugnant to [Eisenhower] of all his acts in his eight years in the White House."

It might be noted that in all the cases discussed, the effectiveness of judicial restraints on Presidents has depended on the willingness of the Presidents themselves to comply with the courts. The courts themselves command practically no resources capable of coercing a President. When the Supreme Court ruled that Nixon had to turn over the Watergate tapes, many people speculated about what measures could be taken if Nixon refused to comply. Nixon did obey the Court in the end, however, and even Franklin Roosevelt at the height of his popularity obeyed the Court, because the American public made it clear it would not tolerate a President who defied a Supreme Court order. To this extent, then, the power of the Supreme Court and of other federal courts rests mainly with American citizens, who believe that Presidents should comply with the laws of the United States as interpreted by the Supreme Court.

IMPEACHMENT

The Constitution provides that a President may be impeached for "treason, bribery, or other high crimes and misdemeanors." The framers of the Constitution evidently intended this phrase to cover more than only crimes punishable by ordinary courts of law. They obviously also meant to include offenses resulting from "the abuse or violation of some public trust," as the *Federalist Papers*—a group of essays written by some of the Convention delegates to win support for the new Constitution—explained. Articles of impeachment are to be drawn up by the House of Representatives. Impeachment proceedings are to take place in the Senate, with the Chief Justice of the Supreme Court presiding. A two-thirds vote is required for conviction. Convicted Presidents would be removed from office and remain criminally liable for offenses they may have committed while in office.

Until Watergate and the move to impeach President Nixon began in 1973, most students of American government believed that impeachment of a President was impractical and unlikely ever to occur. It was thought that if a President were ever impeached and convicted, no future President would attempt to defy Congress. In other words, impeachment meant the destruction of the Presidency. It was also thought that members of Congress would avoid impeaching a President out of fear that they would be accused of engaging in partisan politics.

These beliefs originated because of the impeachment trial of Andrew Johnson. Johnson, a Democrat, was Lincoln's Vice-President and became President when Lincoln was assassinated. For most of his Administration, Johnson was at odds with the radical Republicans in Congress over how to accomplish the reconstruction of the South. Congress tried to limit Johnson's activities as much as possible and finally impeached him for refusing to carry out some of its policies. The Senate failed to convict Johnson by one vote, and in subsequent years the radicals were widely blamed for their partisan behavior.

This condemnation of the Johnson impeachment process was somewhat unfair. The specific charges against Johnson were poorly drawn up, but many historians now believe that the radicals were not simply playing partisan politics in their impeachment of Johnson. Because of Johnson's leniency toward the South, many ex-slaves died and racial injustices were permitted to continue that the radicals wanted to abolish. Nevertheless, the unfavorable view of the impeachment trial was so widely shared that there were no efforts to start impeachment proceedings against Johnson's presidential successors for over a century.

When the Watergate crisis developed, Congress still did not rush to draw up charges for impeachment. The enormous prestige Nixon enjoyed as chief of state made many people feel that impeaching him would be seen as disgracing the country. However, as the public became more and more suspicious of Nixon and more and more demanding of a full investigation of the scandal, the House of Representatives began to collect evidence and slowly built a case for impeachment. Nixon finally resigned when it became obvious that the House would impeach him and the Senate would convict him and remove him from office.

The Watergate Affair showed that impeachment was an effective part of the system of checks and balances, but it also raised some important questions about the nature of the impeachment power. Nixon's defenders argued that impeachment was possible only if the President personally broke the law. By their reasoning, neither the actions of the President's aides nor any actions of the President that were not specific violations of criminal law were sufficient grounds for impeachment. In the actual case, these issues became irrelevant because evidence was made public which showed that Nixon personally did break the law by obstructing justice. However, it is not likely that future impeachment trials will be able to count on evidence as indisputable as Nixon's White House tapes, and it is conceivable that the questions raised by the Affair will come up again.

Let us consider, therefore, some imaginary cases. Suppose that a Cabinet officer is taking advantage of his or her position to extort money from some businessmen. This would not be hard to do, because government regulations affect so many companies. Rumors of these extortions are published by a newspaper. A few days later, the President says that the charges have been investigated and have been found to be untrue. Later, the Cabinet officer is indicted by a grand jury, and it is discovered that the President never really investigated. Should the President be impeached?

In this case, the President's defenders might argue that the President had been misled by the Cabinet officer but had personally committed no crime worthy of impeachment. The Constitution, however, did not intend the impeachment power to be used only against criminals but against any President who proved to be incapable of handling the responsibilities of the office. As we have seen, one of the main responsibilities of the President is supervising the rest of the executive branch, and there is no doubt that the founding fathers expected that Presidents who were lax in this duty would be impeached. In the First Congress, for example, Madison argued that the President ought to be given the power to remove officers of the executive branch. The advantage of this, he said, was that it made the President responsible to the public for the conduct of the person he had nominated and appointed. Madison believed that any President who permitted subordinates to abuse their office would be subject to the decisive engine of impeachment.

In our hypothetical case, therefore, Congress would have to decide whether the President had made an honest effort to prevent corruption—in the words of the Constitution, had the President "taken care" to enforce the laws? Congress would unquestionably have the right to ignore any claims of executive privilege in order to find out what had happened. If it found the President had been careless or gullible, Congress could vote for impeachment even if the President had not committed a crime.

Suppose now, that a President has ordered a military expedition without getting a declaration of war. Many people on both sides die as a result. The President claims that national security was at stake, but not everybody believes it. Should the President be impeached?

In this case, the question Congress would have to decide is whether national security really was in immediate danger. It would again have the right to get all the facts about the case. If it decided that there was no real danger, it would have the right to impeach. The White House is no place for someone who acts hastily or unwisely when human lives are at stake, however well intentioned the person who orders that action may be. Congress could also impeach if it felt there had been time for the President to consult it and get its formal approval, since by failing to do this the President had usurped powers given to Congress by the Constitution.

In general, then, Congress can impeach the President whenever it believes the President is not efficient, wise, or honest enough to perform the duties of the office. There is no need for the President to commit a crime; it is enough that presidential power is abused or that public confidence in the government is threatened by the President's remaining in office. This may seem a harsh rule, but then the power of impeachment was meant to be used for the protection of the country and not the maintenance in office of specific individuals.

There is little danger, however, that the impeachment power will be abused by Congress. Impeachment is conceivable only when there is overwhelming public sentiment for removing the President—in a sense it is as much a tool of public opinion as it is of the Congress. For this reason, although impeachment proved effective in dealing with the Watergate Affair, the likelihood is that Congress will continue to be very cautious, perhaps overly cautious, in employing it.

POSTSCRIPT: THE VICE-PRESIDENCY

The Vice-Presidency is something of an anomaly in American government. On the one hand, the Vice-President has almost no power and very little influence. The only constitutional authority of the office is the right to preside over the Senate. The President may choose to give the Vice-President additional duties, but in practice these duties are usually ceremonial, such as being the President's representative abroad or in the United States. The Vice-Presidency is, in fact, so weak that many previously important politicians lost most of their power and independence when they became Vice-President. John Nance Garner, who retired as Speaker of the House of Representatives to serve as Franklin Roosevelt's first Vice-President, later described the office as "not worth a pitcher of warm spit." Lyndon Johnson and Hubert Humphrey, who were both prominent Democratic party leaders in the Senate, virtually disappeared from sight while they were Vice-President. And when President Eisenhower was asked what important decisions Vice-President Richard Nixon had helped make, he answered that if he were given a few days, he might be able to think of one.

So far, in the twentieth century the only real exception to this rule has been Jimmy Carter's Vice-President, Walter Mondale. In the early years of Carter's Administration, Mondale has played an important role in setting both domestic and foreign policies. He was a major influence in setting up new regulations concerning the FBI's and CIA's authority to conduct surveillance on U.S. citizens, and he helped establish the Administration's position on a case before the Supreme Court concerning "affirmative action" for minorities in university admissions programs. In foreign affairs, Mondale contributed to establishing U.S. policy in the Mideast, and he participated in the negotiations with the Soviet Union to limit the proliferation of dangerous strategic weapons.

Mondale's authority, however, came from his close relationship with President Carter, not from the Vice-Presidency. He was influential because Carter respected his judgment and was willing to listen to his advice. One of Carter's highest White House aides commented about Mondale that "No one inside or outside the Administration has more impact on Jimmy Carter." It was as an adviser to Carter more than as Vice-President that Mondale had access to any documents he wished to see and could attend any meeting he was interested in.

There are some advantages to being Vice-President, however. Vice-Presidents are constitutionally in line to become President if the office becomes vacant, and they are also in a position to win their party's presidential nomination when the President they serve finishes office. Of the Presidents between Franklin Roosevelt and Gerald Ford, only two, Eisenhower and Kennedy, were elected without having been Vice-President first. Presidents Truman and Johnson became President by the death of their predecessors, and President Ford by Nixon's resignation. Nixon himself owed his success partially to his position as Vice-President under Eisenhower. In addition, both Hubert Humphrey in 1968 and Nixon in 1960 were their party's nominees for President after having served as Vice-President. Vice-Presidents, therefore, have dominated the selection of Presidents for more than thirty years.

The significance of the Vice-Presidency in presidential politics is made more serious by the way Vice-Presidents are chosen. The usual method is for a party's presidential nominee to name the Vice-President after winning the nomination, and this choice is ratified by the convention. Generally, the presidential nominees are more concerned with winning the election than with selecting a successor, and they often choose running mates who are relatively unknown or undistinguished but who "balance" the ticket in some way—by being from a different region, having a different religion, or representing a different wing of their own party, for example. This practice sometimes results in individuals becoming President who would never have been chosen President in a general election. For this reason, the Vice-Presidency constitutes a weakness in the office of the Presidency itself.

BIBLIOGRAPHY

Beard, Charles A. *The Presidents in American History*. Rev. ed. New York: Messner, 1977.

Binkley, Wilfred E. *The Powers of the President: Problems of American Democracy*. New York: Russell, 1973.

Commanger, Henry S. *The Defeat of America: Presidential Power & the National Character*. New York: Simon & Schuster, 1975.

* Cooke, Donald E. *Atlas of the Presidents*. Rev. ed. New Jersey: Hammond Inc., 1976.

Corwin, Edward S. *The President: Office & Powers*. 4th rev. ed. New York: NYU Press, 1974.

Fincher, Ernest B. *The Presidency: An American Invention*. New York: Abelard, 1977.

Goldsmith, William M. *The Growth of Presidential Power: A Documented History*, 3 vols. New York: Bowker, 1975.

Hargrove, Erwin C. *The Power of the Modern Presidency*. Pennsylvania: Temple U. Press, 1974.

James, Dorothy B. *The Contemporary Presidency*. 2nd ed. New York: Pegasus, 1974.

* Johnson, Gerald W. *The Presidency*. Fisher, Leonard E., illus. New York: Morrow, 1962.

Kurland, Gerald. *The Growth of Presidential Power*. New York: SamHar Press, 1974.

Liston, Robert. *Presidential Power: How Much Is Too Much?* New York: McGraw Hill, 1971.

* Lovelace, Delos W. *Ike Eisenhower: Statesman & Soldier of Peace*. Rev. ed. New York: T. Y. Crowell, 1969.

Masters, Nicholas A. and Baluss, Mary E. *The Growing Powers of the Presidency: A Background Book for Young People*. New York: Parents Press, 1970.

Morgan, Ruth P. *President and Civil Rights: Policy-Making by Executive Order*. New York: St. Martin's Press, 1970.

* Mothner, Ira. *Woodrow Wilson, Champion of Peace*. New York: Franklin Watts, 1969.

Weingast, David E. *We Elect a President*. Rev. ed. New York: Messner, 1977.

White, Theodore H. *Making of the President*. New York: Atheneum, 1961.

Wibberley, Leonard. *Man of Liberty: A Life of Thomas Jefferson*. Rev. ed. New York: Farrar Straus & Giroux, 1968.

* Indicates books geared to younger readers.

ABOUT THE AUTHOR

Charles Radding is an assistant professor of history at Loyola University in Chicago. Mr. Radding, a native of Massachusetts, did his undergraduate work at the University of Chicago and received a Ph.D. from Princeton University. He has previously taught at Lewis and Clark College in Portland, Oregon, and at Herbert H. Lehman College of the City University of New York.